America Smiles

Hal Raymond

VANTAGE PRESS
New York

FIRST EDITION

Copyright © 1998 by Hal Raymond

Published by Vantage Press, Inc.
516 West 34th Street, New York, New York 10001

Manufactured in the United States of America
ISBN: 0-533-12489-1

Library of Congress Catalog Card No.: 97-90806

0 9 8 7 6 5 4 3 2 1

To my children,
Carol and Kenneth, who sustain me,
and to the memory of
May and Kenneth, who danced with me

*This is not a story of high-priced stars
—but rather a story of thousands of
journeymen performers who made their
living in the variety show business by being
there and doing their thing during the dark
days of the Depression . . .*

—Hal Raymond

*"But observe, sire, how
they light up the sky. . . . "*

—Shakespeare

Author's Note

An ounce of freedom is worth a pound of promises.

It is upon this simple principle that the events in this book took place.

Only in this country, and in the period this book covers, could great numbers of people who called themselves variety entertainers, comedians, singers, dancers, orchestra musicians, and whatever, travel great distances across our country without interference, back and forth, back and forth and up and down as they chose.

With the exception of our Canadian friends and their friendship, this freedom was not possible anywhere else in the world. And it is this period (roughly from 1929 to 1940) that we rely on most heavily for the expression of freedom America took for granted until we saw how quickly other countries lost it.

Taking shows and entertainment and enjoyment to every nook and cranny of our great country helped to keep the American spirit strong and helped us prepare for the terrible war that had to be fought in Europe.

When we talk about entertainment in peacetime, it seems a frivolous subject, but when things got dark and people had to be cheered up, when jokes had to be told, when songs had to be written and played and sung and danced to, as they were in the Variety Theatre, a kind of emotional magnet was created that helped pull our country together and helped us focus on doing what had to be done in those frightening days.

It is in an effort to describe, in a lighthearted manner and through my eyes, the wonderful people who surrounded me and my dear brother, Ken, and my wife, May, as we played scores of variety theatres and supper clubs in an era of life and death, of laughter and tears, of hate and love, that we struggled in to do our bit in helping to keep our native optimism alive.

The events and people that are referred to are all real; all events took place and I relay them to you in a spirit of proud association.

So — here's to America and the spirit of freedom that allowed us to do those things and to the special people who had the special talents to meet the needs that the Variety Theatre answered so completely when it was called upon to help America remember what it was fighting for.

> —Hal Raymond (the stage name for
> Harry C. Raymond)
> Orange, Connecticut 1998

Contents

The night was bright
With the full moon's light
It was Halloween—it was October 1929
A bad month for Fridays. . . .

It was only the beginning.
    —Hal Raymond

Reed and Duthers

It all began in Cincinnati in the 1920s.

I was working for a chain of dry cleaners called Fenton's. I was about 13 or so. I would pick up the finished dry cleaning, the suits and coats and dresses and so forth and carry them to their various destinations in downtown Cincinnati. I was humiliated by this job. I would pass other kids and they'd be walking along freely, laughing and talking together and I'd be struggling with bundles of cleaning, some I carried in bags, some on hangers across my shoulders.

One day as I was walking slowly down the street, hoping no one would recognize me as I was trying to keep the cleaning from slipping and falling to the sidewalk, I saw a poster that said the Palace Theatre was running what was then a new idea: moving pictures with a live stage show afterwards. I was so disgusted with my job I stopped to read the poster. It said there would be a dancing act. I thought to myself, I wonder what that looks like.

It cost 50 cents to get in the theatre. I carried the cleaning with me, dumped it in the seat alongside me and sat back to see what would happen. The moving picture had just ended in this great big beautiful theatre. Suddenly the lights came up, the orchestra came into view, the stage lights came on, the music started, the curtain opened and then from out of the wings came Reed and Duthers, two very dashing looking young men in identical suits dancing identical steps.

I was amazed. They were tap dancing. As I listened to

1

them and watched them, I became enchanted, really entranced. I was, you might say, entrapped for life. I was so fascinated by the expression of rhythm that my whole body was actually trembling with joy. I never imagined a thing like that could happen.

After watching Reed and Duthers and the crisp execution of their dance steps and the way they looked, I said to myself as I picked up the rumpled dry cleaning, That's what I'm going to do some day. Some day I'm going to dance like that.

I was so excited about the prospect of dancing and talked about it so much that my brother, Ken, who was a year older than I, decided he might as well try it, too. With money we continued to earn from a variety of jobs, Ken and I took tap dancing lessons from a young man who was an exceptionally good teacher, especially for beginners. His name was George Geisler. He and his mother operated a dancing school which featured tap dancing, although they taught other types of dancing as well.

I was amazed at how easily tap dancing came to me. I learned the steps quickly and almost effortlessly. After a while, Ken and I switched over to a school that was tremendously successful in Cincinnati at the time, the Schuster-Martin School of Theatre. It had produced top people such as Tyrone Power, Libby Holman who was queen of the blues, Evelyn Venable who was the leading Shakespearean actress, and others.

By enrolling there, we came under the tutelage of a true theatrical genius, Paul Batchelor. He was of medium height, with brown hair and a strong, graceful appearance. He could do anything and everything when it came to putting a show together. Although he had studied ballet since a child, he said to me, "I'm not going to give you ballet lessons. I don't want you to look like a ballet dancer

2

when you're up there. I want you to look like you do ordinarily, so we'll concentrate on the things you will probably use the most in your routines such as turns, which are always necessary."

So we worked on turns until I was able to do a couple of turns in the air, which was quite acrobatic, and was able to land in the right position to segue into flash turns on the order of what Michael Jackson does today. My routine would usually start with a couple of turns in the air and on landing I would go into eight or ten flash turns. It made me feel heroic before my routine even started.

As time went on, we became more and more proficient, although Ken was never as interested in dancing as he was in other aspects of the variety theatre, especially comedy. Eventually, in my opinion, he became as good a straight man and light comedian as Bud Abbott, who was regarded as the best straight man in the business, and rightfully so. He was the foil for Lou Costello in their famous act that everyone knew as "Abbott and Costello."

Ken's first break as a talking actor came when he finally got a small role in a show; in fact, his role was so small it consisted of just one line. He was to come on the stage and say to the leading man, "Dammit all, Nolan." He was so proud of his line, his first speaking line on the stage, that he practiced it hundreds of times around our house. It became a family joke. We kidded him constantly because his renditions would be different each time. One would be, "Dammit . . . all . . . Nolan," or "Dam . . . mit . . . all, Nolan," or "Dammit . . . all, Nolan." He'd keep asking us which one we thought was the best. Finally, after several weeks of this he was satisfied with his interpretation. When he came on stage he was a huge success for a one-line actor.

As time went on, we were hooked for good. We were both marked for the variety theatre. In our new found profession we were so overjoyed to be in that atmosphere with the prospect of someday even getting paid for it that we were overwhelmed. We rehearsed constantly.

Eventually, Paul Batchelor, the guiding genius in our lives, was contracted by Radio Keith Orpheum—commonly known as RKO, the biggest force in stage productions at the time to stage a show in Cincinnati. As far as I know, this may have been the first time RKO had decided to produce a show outside of New York or Hollywood.

Paul Batchelor was commissioned to produce a show called "Manhattan Serenade." It was a beautiful musical comedy. It had its own original book and score, and with Paul in charge the choreography was the best it could be. He made the costumes, he directed us in our dancing and speaking roles, and guided us and the rest of the cast in doing whatever was necessary.

After weeks of rehearsals and a week's break-in engagement in Cincinnati, "Manhattan Serenade" was booked by RKO for a 90-week run with performances first in New York City and then with appearances in RKO theatres throughout the country. It was a true "tone poem," an art form that was on the leading edge of entertainment for large shows in the variety theatre at the time. It combined music, dance and dialogue in a fresh theatrical manner similar to how "West Side Story" would be produced later on, as well as those shows produced by the Gershwin brothers.

Ken and I were among the 50 talented young people in the cast of "Manhattan Serenade" who had been aspiring show business students at the Schuster-Martin School of Theatre. We were all leaving for New York City by different means of transportation. It was the most exciting time in their lives and certainly in ours. We were embroiled in the variety theatre for good.

There were seven young people in our group, including the driver, as we set out in an old dark blue La Salle with our baggage strapped on top for 700 miles of bad roads.

When we first started out I suddenly became so homesick for home and mother that I persuaded the driver to stop the car after we had only gone ten miles. He said, "We can't do this, we'll never get there." I said, "Just do it this one time." So from ten miles away, in a little town called Milford, Ohio, I got out, called my mother and told her how lonesome I was. I was only 17 and this was the first time I had been away from home. I got back in the car and we were off and running.

Later on, as we were wheeling through Pennsylvania, the brakes caught fire due to our overloaded car. We were trailing flames behind us when the state police came roaring up on motorcycles to stop us. We got out of the car, they hosed down the brakes with a fire extinguisher, we got back in and continued on our way.

Since it was the first time I had ever been on my own, I ordered my two favorite foods for breakfast: pumpkin pie with chocolate ice cream à la mode.

Our driver, who liked to kid us, kept up a steady stream of warnings about what we should do when we got to the big city. Particularly, he told us to be sure the windows were closed tight when we went through the Holland tunnel so water wouldn't get into the car. Eventually we got to New York City and registered at the Somerset Hotel at 47th and Broadway.

Although we didn't know it, we had started our big adventure on Halloween night, October 1929, the date of the stock market crash and the start of the worst depression our country has ever experienced. We had no idea what "a stock market crash" meant, but we were soon to learn how profound an effect this would have upon our lives and upon the lives of millions of people throughout the world.

As we were getting out of the car and unloading our bags at the Somerset, we heard two short muscular men arguing on the sidewalk about who between them had ruined their act at the Palace the night before. One said to the other, "You know that tinsika didn't go there. You did it in the wrong place."

"No, I didn't," said the other as they walked away arguing.

Later we learned that they were acrobats and that the "tinsika" was a spectacular acrobatic maneuver that consisted of a horizontal turn in the air switching from one foot to the other at high speed. Audiences loved it and always applauded wildly.

Newspapers at the time were full of news about gangsters and we had a taste of it. We had been in our room on the third floor of the Somerset Hotel about 20 minutes when we heard the staccato bark of tommy guns. We looked out the window, and sure enough, we saw a man lying on the sidewalk, apparently he had been shot, "rubbed out" as they said in the papers. The police came and took him away. Nobody asked any questions. And that was the end of that.

The next day, our first day in New York, was our Number One day in the variety theatre. We were called to a meeting of the cast of "Manhattan Serenade." And then we were told.

Our distinguished producer, director, composer and choreographer, Paul Batchelor, told us that because of the stock market crash, our 90-week run had been cut down to nine weeks. That was our first taste of show business in big time variety theatre. Needless to say, we were all stunned and looked at each other in dismay.

The next three days saw rapid developments on the down side. Our nine weeks had been cut down to one week. We played our one week and then went to see Mr. George Godfrey who a short time before had been the distinguished looking, powerful booker for the RKO circuit. But now he only had about three weeks at this command. He said, "This is it fellas. We gotta wait and see what develops."

So, we were off and running on our own in New York City. Laughing, we thought, all the way.

Whose feet were hard to beat—in dancing—or
running down the street (backwards).
                                    —Hal Raymond

Bojangles (Bill Robinson)

Ken and I had not been in New York very long when we
were excited to see Bill Robinson's name on the marquee of
a theatre on 42nd Street announcing that Bill Robinson
(Bojangles) was headlining in a show called "Brown Bud-
dies." Bojangles was our idol. No one could dance like
Bojangles. We had always wanted to see him and because it
was a matinee we thought we might be able to get in.

So, with the innocence and self-assurance of youth (we
were only 17 and 18 at the time), we went around to the
stage door and asked to see Mr. Robinson. When he came,
we were so green we showed him our tap shoes and said to
him, "You see, Mr. Robinson, we're tap dancers, also. We
would love to see you dance. Can you extend us professional courtesy?"

He looked at us as though we had just come down
from Mars. We held our shoes out to him with the soles up
to show the metal taps. Bojangles studied them seriously
for a moment, and then with a big, wide smile he looked up
and said, "Okay, boys. I'll call the box office and see what
they can do." And then he added, "Just to let you know,
when I dance, my shoes have wooden soles and heels."

We went out to the box office, and sure enough, Bojangles had called and ordered two wonderful seats for us
right in the middle of the first row where we could watch
him directly. Bojangles even made an announcement saying this was a special occasion because two friends of his

had dropped by and he was going to have Pig Meat Markham play the piano for him while he danced. It was a marvelous duo. We wondered how Pig Meat Markham's piano playing could sound so marvelous—then we noticed he had a tap on one heel and he kept tapping that heel in time with the music. The effect—his playing the piano and tapping his heel while Bill Robinson danced—was really overwhelming. Bojangles did use wooden soles and heels on his shoes that are also traditional with Lancaster clog and Irish step dancers. I just want to say "thanks" to a great man, a great dancer and a great human being. Thank you, again, Bojangles.

Bill Robinson had another talent not many people knew about: He was considered one of the world's fastest, if not the fastest, backwards runner of his day.

One lazy summer afternoon in New York an idea took hold as sometimes happens in the Big Apple. One word led to another and suddenly a 50-yard foot race was announced to take place at 42nd and Broadway between Bojangles—running backwards—and a world class sprinter.

Bill Robinson was given a 20-yard start. Everybody lined up. A large crowd had gathered. The runners were off—and sure enough—Bojangles, running backwards, finished a step or two ahead of the guy who had given him a 20-yard lead.

Everyone cheered. Traffic had been stopped. It was a big impromptu celebration. Even then, it was highly unusual to see a foot race in the middle of the street at 42nd and Broadway. Can you imagine this happening today!

It's a good thing for the wide receivers and tight ends playing in the National Football League today that Bill Robinson is not playing free safety. No one could ever complete a pass over his head the way he could run backwards.

A little bit of Americana.

Catch as catch can was steady work. . . .
—Hal Raymond

Boyhood to Manhood

We grew up pretty fast after our 90-week run on the RKO circuit disappeared into the mists of the depression. We were a long way from home, we didn't have a job and we didn't have a dime. The three of us, Ken and I and Charlie Fey—also from Cincinnati, who was a member of the "Manhattan Serenade" cast—were really stranded. We needed a friend. That friend turned out to be more than a friend: He was a guardian angel. His name was Billy Silvers.

Billy had been a longtime friend of our Aunt Kate. He was a born and bred New Yorker, a big husky good-natured man who was convinced, like the majority of New Yorkers at the time, that anything west of the Hudson River was full of covered wagons and cowboys. Aunt Kate had lived in New York for about 20 years and considered it her home town. When she and Billy heard of our predicament, they began to treat us with the good-hearted New Yorkishness so prevalent in New York in those times.

Billy picked us up at the Somerset Hotel and, believe it or not, we sat in his car at the corner of 47th and Broadway—and no one ever asked us to move—for several hours while we listened to Billy formulate his generous plan. He got out a pad and pencil and wrote down how much it would cost for the three of us to eat breakfast, lunch and dinner at midtown restaurants. We could also get a complete Chinese dinner at a Chinese restaurant for 25 cents, including a fortune cookie for dessert.

Billy gave us the money and said he would keep on

giving it until we got on our feet. I think he really liked being able to talk about show business with us and I suspect he had a little bit of Al Jolson and Eddie Cantor in his makeup.

We began immediately to make the rounds of booking agents. Most of them were located in the Bond Building or in the Brill Building, which were about a block apart from each other right in the center of the Broadway scene.

Sometimes we would go through our routines about three feet in front of the bookers, mostly men, who invariably were clean-shaven but always had a bluish cast to their faces. We called them "blue jowls." When I was doing my routine, they would stare at me in a way that reminded me of a racehorse auction, as though they were measuring me and saying, "Could this horse really do six furlongs in 1:08?"

Making the rounds as we did every day resulted in a lucky break. It put us in touch with a wonderful agent. His name was Henry Weiss. He was truly a gentleman and had a vast knowledge of variety show business coupled with that fortunate knack of who to call for what and where.

Our beloved Aunt Kate would prove to be our "ace in the hole" as long as we were in New York. She was a marvelous cook, and whenever things got tough and as long as we could pony up a nickel to call her and another nickel to ride the subway to Forest Hills, Long Island, where she lived, she would always cook us a wonderful dinner. She did this on and off for years and fed many of our show business friends who were "at liberty." She always ended her telephone conversation with "And don't be late."

Our first job was on a four-day variety bill in Bound Brook, New Jersey. We were part of a bill that included Les Caulfield, a popular Irish step dancer, and his wife, a beautiful blonde acrobatic dancer. We began picking up jobs fairly often and were becoming more and more self confident. We rehearsed every spare minute. All of a sudden we became glossy, glamourous young men with a youthful show business glow and made the successful change from bewildered boys to professional young performers.

She wanted to be as sophisticated as the other girls.
　　　　　　　　　　　　　　　　—Hal Raymond

The Glance

Taking big variety theatre shows on the road was an enormous undertaking. So much had to be done; so many people had to be at the ready for costumes, lights, sets, and music; so many performers had to be rehearsed and cued; so many advance men and ticket agents had to be notified; and so many theatres had to be reserved. Thus, men and women had to live and work and perform together and so it was natural for liaisons to develop, that steady friendships would become the stuff of gossip. Sometimes hearts were bruised or bent or broken. There weren't many secrets between cast and crew.

Beautiful girls, of course, helped hold it all together. After they had been on the road for a while, living in this closed intense atmosphere, chorus girls became fairly sophisticated, worldly. Or so it seemed to younger girls who joined the cast.

I had finished rehearsing late one night and was having a cup of coffee before going up to a room reserved for me. Sometimes, only occasionally, we were assigned rooms when we were going to be with the show for only a short time. I looked up and there was the most beautiful young girl of all. Apparently she had just joined the cast as one of the resident chorus girls. I had only seen her briefly in the past few days. Holy smoke, she was so young and so pretty! I was really only about 20 or so, but I felt like a grizzly old timer. She couldn't have been more than 16 or 17.

She had a cup of coffee in her hand and looked at me inquiringly. I said, loftily, "Please, sit down." As she sat

14

across from me, she studied me with wide blue innocent eyes, as though she were trying to make up her mind about something. "Do you have a girl?" she asked. I said, truthfully, "No. Not at the moment." She held the coffee cup with both hands and looked over the rim at me with a glance that was direct and almost childlike.

"I'm glad."

I finished my coffee. It was getting very late and I had an early morning rehearsal. "Do you know where you're staying?" I asked, for want of anything else to say.

"Not really."

"Well, look. Why don't I find out?" I went over to the back wall and pretended to look at the assignment board knowing full well what my room number was but not having a clue as to what hers might be. When I got back to the table, she was gone. I took the elevator up to my room and was surprised to see the door open. She was sitting on the bed looking confused and nervous with my door keys in her hand. She tried several times to speak, but had a hard time swallowing, and no words came out. She couldn't take her eyes off her hands and the keys as she clasped and unclasped them on her lap. I was totally at a loss.

"Do you want something?" I asked.

That's when she started to cry. "I'm doing this all wrong," she said. "I heard girls talking tonight about how they, I mean, when they . . . sort of like someone . . . and want to be with . . . be with someone . . . they, they, they just say so," she blurted out.

The light came on in my head. Of course. I doubt that anyone would have believed me if I told them what happened the rest of the week. I was surprised myself.

She came to my room every night wearing some kind of a short thing that looked like a slip. I wore pajamas for the first time in my life, a Christmas present from my mother. We slept together, spoon fashion like babes in the wood, my arm around her waist, all in chaste and innocent purity.

I noticed several times during the following days that she would be in a group of older girls talking and laughing. Occasionally one would look over at me and smile knowingly. Now she was one of the girls, and the glance she gave me confirmed it.

I had to leave at the end of the week. So, just before I left, with everyone standing around, I bent over and kissed her. For the first time, I might add. On the train heading toward my next engagement I smiled to myself. Now she was one of the girls. I didn't even know her name.

The many hearts of New York City.
　　　　—Hal Raymond

Our Neighborhood—51st and 8th Avenue

Ken and I lived for a while at the Landseer Apartments at 51st and 8th with a lot of other people in the variety theatre. We were all struggling to survive in the midst of the depression and many of us—with the generous help of merchants in our neighborhood—had worked out a pretty comfortable living pattern.

I will always remember the friendly proprietor of a huge newsstand at the corner of 51st and 8th Avenue. He knew we were broke so he'd let us take whatever magazines or newspapers we wanted, and if we didn't fold them or get them dirty we could take them back when we were through with them. In the meantime, we had run up a bill with the neighborhood grocery store and were paying it as best we could. One day we told him how sorry we were that we owed him $400. He said, "Let me tell you something, boys." He said he was trying to collect from some of the biggest names in show business who owed him as much as $8,000. "I'm not worried about you guys. I know you'll pay me sooner or later."

In the meantime, we had built up enough credit at the Landseer Apartments so we didn't have to worry about a place to live. So, all in all, we had worked out a pretty good living pattern. We had all of the latest magazines and newspapers we wanted to read, we had what food we could afford to eat, and we had a place to live.

I must mention, however, the famous Horn and Hardart restaurants, especially the one we frequented right

17

on Broadway in Manhattan. It was between 47th and 48th. If you had a nickel for a cup of coffee, you knew there would always be some catsup and crackers on the table. The manager would look the other way while we heaped catsup on the crackers. It kept what we called "The Broadway Beach Front" alive by the manager's generosity and kindness of heart. People would stagger out of there full of catsup and crackers and be able to keep going.

So, here's the tip of my hat to great acts of kindness in a great city which are probably forgotten by everyone except those variety performers who remembered and lived by them. So thank you, Horn and Hardart and all of the other neighborhood shopkeepers who had faith in us and our good word.

Great beauty and great tragedy go hand in hand when men flout the law of brotherly love.

—Hal Raymond

46th and Broadway

As a sign of the times, I remember one beautiful early spring morning when I was out walking seeing New York at its prettiest after a late night party in Harlem. I was standing at the corner of 46th and Broadway when I felt, rather than saw, something unusual. I thought I saw a shadow. I looked up and there was the *Hindenburg*, silhouetted against a purple and peach-colored sky sailing majestically and silently to its rendezvous with the mooring mast in Lakehurst, New Jersey.

I thought to myself how wonderful—little did I know that I was looking at the harbinger of terror and death that was to come in a few weeks. It was on May 6, 1937, that the *Hindenburg* came to its tragic end. But on that morning it was an awe-inspiring sight as it went on to moor uneventfully at Lakehurst.

I mention it because the *Hindenburg* had been making regular transatlantic flights from Germany for about a year. Its silent hovering over the city had become part of the New York scene.

19

Sometimes even the best can't take what they dish out.
—Hal Raymond

Backstage Days—in the Variety Theatre

Among the performers of great talent in the variety theatre we encountered along the way were Pat Rooney and his son, billed as Pat Rooney III.

Pat Rooney was king of the waltz clog and soft shoe. He did everything just right. His routine was just right. The music was just right—especially the music that then symbolized, and still does today, the soul of New York: "The Sidewalks of New York." When Pat Rooney, dancing the waltz clog without taps, swung into "East Side, West Side, All Around the Town," the audience couldn't get enough of it. Of course horse racing fans will recognize the song as it is played today before the big race known as the Belmont, the last jewel of the Triple Crown horse races.

Pat Rooney's son, Pat Rooney III, was also a talented dancer. He did a style of dancing that was briefly very big in America. It was called "Frisco" dancing. I don't know where the name came from. But it was a gliding, eccentric kind of dancing, highly individualized. Very much like the way Michael Jackson dances today without an ensemble.

In contrast to the advanced tap dancing at the time—known as offbeat rhythm dancing whose main thrust was to make a joyous noise with a lot of action—you could dance full bore in Frisco dancing and your hat would stay on.

As an interesting sideline, some may remember that George Raft, the famous actor who played in numerous gangster movies, started out as a Frisco dancer. Apparently his ability to keep his hat on while dancing impressed Hollywood agents. When Frisco style dancing went out of vogue, George Raft turned to the hot subject of gangsterism, still with his hat on, and turned his habit of tossing a quarter in the air and catching it repeatedly into his movie trademark.

Pat Rooney III also did a wonderful routine known as "Hitting the Bottle." The song came from Earl Carroll's "Vanities" and was introduced by a trio of dancers known as Wells, Mordecai and Taylor. Pat Rooney III picked it up along with others who added their own interpretations to it.

About this time, Ken and I and our partner, Charlie Fey, were getting ready for a theatrical debut all alone and not cradled in the arms of a big musical comedy. We were going to open in a place called Bound Brook, New Jersey, a well-known metropolis (I use the word with tongue in cheek) known at the time as the place for breaking in new entertainers in the variety theatre. It was a four day split week engagement. We suffered great anxiety and practiced constantly.

Unfortunately, our dressing room was right over the one occupied by Pat Rooney. Eventually, he came out in the hall and yelled up to us, "Holy Smoke, fellas. Keep on practicing, because you need it. But don't practice over people's heads!" That was the way we said goodbye to Pat Rooney and Pat Rooney III. Pat gave us a publicity photo of himself and wrote on it, "You boys are great. You have nothing to worry about. Continue to practice. But not over my head!"

No times are too tough for a true Irish heart.
—Hal Raymond

Mrs. Murphy's Rooming House

Ken and I answered an ad in the paper that read, "Furnished Rooms for Rent." It turned out to be a double front brownstone building between 8th and 9th on 51st Street. Mrs. Murphy, the owner and operator, opened the door. We were too immature to realize at the time what a really nice person she was. She was truly an Irish angel.

She took a look at us and decided to rent us a huge front room on the second floor with two beds. She said, "Well boys. I have very few rules here. If you're hungry, I'll be glad to feed you, but you have to be ready on time. I try to keep a clean religious house." Of course we said yes to everything.

We lived there for several months. She gave us breakfast sitting around a big table in the kitchen. Although she had other tenants, we were the only ones she gave breakfast to. Ken and I were with two other friends, Roger Logan and a nice guy from the South, Jack Montgomery. They had rented a room down the hall.

In the middle of the kitchen table was a huge basket of freshly baked New York delicatessen hard rolls, and you know how good they smelled. Some were poppy seed and some were plain. She put out jars of strawberry jam and sweet creamery butter because, she said, "It is healthier for you."

Alongside that basket was another basket almost as big filled with little hand-rolled scrolls on fine quality paper. We had to sit at the table while she said grace and wait for her signal to begin eating which she didn't give until each of us reached into the basket, took out a scroll, unrolled it and read the sayings of the day. For instance, if one said, "The Lord is My Shepherd, I shall not want," she would say, "Oh, you're going to have good luck today."

She would take the scroll, roll it up again and put it back in the basket. By the time all four of us had read the religious saying for the day, and she had finished saying grace, she'd say the magic words we were waiting for: "Okay boys. It's okay to start eating now." Our hands shot out like pistons for the hard rolls and kept going back and forth with blinding speed, faster than an old time Western gunfighter. The basket was empty in about two minutes. We slapped on the butter and jam and drank cup after cup of hot coffee. Then she would say motherly things to us like, "God bless you boys. You're really good boys and you deserve to have good luck today and I think you're going to have it. So I'll see you today as you come and go and I'll say goodnight to you tonight." She did that every day for the several months we stayed there. Needless to say, she was an angel from heaven.

She did another very kind thing. We went to her one day and said some friends of ours didn't have a place to sleep that night and could they stay in our room. We said we could move the beds together lengthwise, if she didn't mind, and there would be room enough for all of us to sleep crosswise.

She said, "Well, okay boys. But you know how we run the house. No rough–housing around. No drinking." We did this several times for friends who had no place to go. One time there were seven sleeping in our room, on the floor, in chairs and crosswise on the beds.

Mrs. Murphy was a classic middle-aged, middle-class Irish flower. Her face when she smiled had the map of Ireland on it. She was of short, ample, motherly stature, and was so generous she had trouble hiding it. As long as she thought you were clean, honest boys, your own mother couldn't have done more for you than she did.

Ken and I were able to pick up considerable work in local vaudeville theatres and began to make a large circle of friends. Things went along this way, day after day. We had our Irish angel as a landlady and a lovely place to live. Things were looking up.

One night, we heard a knock on our door and opened it to see Virginia, one of the young show girls we had spoken to during rehearsals. She seemed very nervous and while she obviously wanted something, she seemed too timid to say so. Finally, after gentle urging, we realized she was asking to borrow some money from us to rent a room to sleep in that night. We said, "Let us talk together for a minute and maybe we can find an answer to your problem." So Ken and I after talking it over said, "Why don't we invite her to stay with us? She can sleep in the single bed by the window and we'll share the big double bed by the door." In the strange camaraderie of the times she gratefully accepted and moved in with Ken and me for the night. We looked upon her as a sisterly comrade in arms and all went to bed.

Suddenly the dark side of life exploded with blinding speed. In the middle of the night we heard heavy pounding on our door. We heard Mrs. Murphy's frightened voice shouting, "Boys! Boys! Get up! Open your door! The house is on fire! You'll have to run for your lives!"

When we started to get out of bed we saw that our floor, which was the ceiling of the floor below, had big holes burned through it. We had to dodge the burning holes even to get to the door. When we opened the door we faced a solid wall of black smoke and could barely make out Mrs. Murphy.

24

Mrs. Murphy, badly frightened but still in control, said, "Just follow me. You know the house. Just hold on to the bannister, if you hold onto it and don't let go, you'll get down all right." We said, "Okay, Mrs. Murphy. You go ahead." She said she wanted to get the people out on the third floor. We said we'd make out okay.

I can still see Ken dodging flames and running back to the closet to get a suit he had bought the day before for $6 at a special sale at Leighton's, a store at 48th and Broadway. He grabbed his suit and started out the door. I had bought a suit at the same time, but he left mine hanging there. I had to grab it on the run. My problem was complicated in that Virginia became panic stricken when she heard Mrs. Murphy shout, "Get out of bed and run for your lives!"

Being an old-fashioned rooming house, the window sills were only about a foot high but the windows themselves were about ten feet high. Virginia jumped up on the windowsill without a stitch on and was clinging to the window frames looking out. By this time a crowd had gathered. In typical New York style they kept yelling up at her just to keep her in the window. "That's a girl. Hang on. Hang on. When the firemen see you, they'll be after you." I jumped on the windowsill behind her, grabbed her around the waist and tried to tug her loose, but she was so panic stricken, so paralyzed with fear and so strong I couldn't get her down. The men on the street kept yelling, "Let her go! Let go of her, you bum! She knows what's she's doing."

Finally I got her to listen to me. "You can't stay here. You'll have to follow me. I'll hold your hand. We're going down stairs. Otherwise you'll die in this fire." I told her I could make it down the stairs even if I couldn't see through the smoke if I held onto the bannister with one hand and held her hand with the other. I clutched my new, precious $6 suit over my lifeline arm holding onto the bannister. I finally told her she simply had to go with me. Now. Now.

That's what she finally did, shaking and sobbing all the way down. At the street level, Mrs. Murphy, who was wearing some kind of a robe over a flannel nightgown, without a word to us, took off the robe and wrapped it around Virginia.

Firemen were rushing around giving oxygen to everyone who needed it.

Mrs. Murphy was so brave she had finally gotten everybody out of the house except the man who had started the fire.

He was in the room right under ours. He often rented the room with his girl friend who Mrs. Murphy always thought was his wife. When the fire broke out in their bed where they had been smoking and drinking the flames shot out into the hallway making it even more dangerous for people trying to get out. We had to wait and run between bursts of flame. Mrs. Murphy didn't know the young woman was there.

But the man knew the house. He knew it well because he had been staying there for a long time. When he saw the fire was out of hand, he jumped down the dumbwaiter shaft, ran out the back of the house and no one ever saw him leave.

We didn't see him; the firemen never saw him. Mrs. Murphy would have recognized him but she didn't see him either. And the poor lady he left there burned to death. It was a terrible tragedy. And Mrs. Murphy never got over it.

We were shocked and sickened at the story when it was revealed to us. The only comedy note came in the midst of the excitement when Mrs. Murphy, carrying her strongbox with all her money in it, went to our room, which surprisingly turned out to be the safest one under the conditions of smoke and flame.

A fireman went up the extension ladder to lead her down. The crowd, which had grown to major proportions by this time, saw that she had the steel box under arm.

Mrs. Murphy and the fireman were both at the top of the extension ladder. The fireman tried to take the box and put it under his arm so he could help Mrs. Murphy down. But she grabbed it back. They had a tug of war at the top of the extension ladder with both of them pulling the strongbox back and forth.

The people on the street who treated it all as a free show were well aware of what Mrs. Murphy probably had in the box. Undoubtedly, most of them had steel strong boxes like it. They yelled encouragement to her: "That's right, Missus. Don't give it to that crook, you'll never see it again. If he wants to take your steel box, he'll have to take you with it."

Finally, the fireman, who undoubtedly was as honest as he was brave, realized he wasn't going to win and carried both Mrs. Murphy and the steel box together down the ladder to the street.

We were all taken to an emergency clinic and treated for smoke inhalation. By late afternoon we were able to get back into the building. Our room had giant round patches where the fire had burned through and we had to walk very gingerly around them to avoid falling through.

When we came back that evening to go to bed a fireman was sitting in our room in a rocking chair reading a newspaper. He said, "Well, fellas, I'll be your companion for a week." He explained that whenever there was a fire of major proportions with a fatality, the Fire Department watched it for a week to be sure there were no embers burning in the walls.

"While you go to sleep," he said, "I'll be sitting here reading the paper all night long until you get up."

We got very friendly with him. We talked a lot about show business and he wondered where the beautiful girl was who was stuck in the window. We said her name was confidential and she was living in her own room now.

We spent a pleasant week with the fireman guarding our room. When it was time for him to leave, it was time for us to leave Mrs. Murphy's also. We were going to open the road show edition of "50 Million Frenchmen" Christmas Eve in Albany the next day.

We traveled to Albany on the famous Hudson River Night Boat, which was an adventure in itself because it was a very stormy night at this time of year.

Practice makes you happier, but never, ever perfect.
                                            —Hal Raymond

Michael's Rehearsal Hall

Our days were spent 10 percent performance and 90 percent rehearsal.

Michael's Rehearsal Hall in Manhattan was the place to go to rehearse. Everyone in the world rehearsed there: dancers, acrobats, comedians, singers, everybody. At any given time great artists of the stature of Paul Draper and Fred Astaire could even be found there.

In all the years I was in the variety theatre there were only two compliments I'm really proud of and that I make so bold as to immodestly describe here. One was at Michael's Rehearsal Hall. The man who took our money at the door and assigned our rehearsal space said to me one day, "I don't have to sign you in, Hal, because I can always tell when you are here by the way you sound." This was high praise, indeed, from a man who heard and watched everybody in the world rehearse constantly and could still know I was there just by the way I sounded and looked when I was rehearsing.

The other compliment occurred at a call for a musical show by the Theatre Guild, the most prestigious dramatic organization in New York City at the time. It was the talk of the street that the Theatre Guild would actually do a musical. It was going to be called "Parade." Ken and I were working at Loew's State at the time and just for laughs we decided to go to the audition.

When it came my turn I danced for Bob Altman, the director. When I finished my routine he seemed in a state of slight shock and said, "Where in the hell did you come from?"

I could have said I just came there between shows at Loew's State, but I said instead, "I just came from Cincinnati, Ohio."

He said, "Don't leave the theatre. You stand right over there."

To me this was the highest praise because there had been scores of people trying out. Some of them I felt sorry for; others I greatly admired, but coming from a man of his professional discrimination to say, "Where in the hell did you come from," was to me high praise indeed. As it turned out, we were lucky not to have been a part of the show because when it finally did open it only lasted a week or so. As a venture, it was a failure and Bob Altman spent the rest of his distinguished directorial career in Hollywood.

This poor food and cold weather will make madmen of us all.
—Shakespeare

Cheese Sandwiches

With more experience under our belts we moved to the Hotel Langwell, one of three hotels on 49th Street in Manhattan that was occupied almost exclusively by professional show people. The other two were the Hotel Chesterfield and the Hotel Plymouth.

It was a tight community of variety show business performers. One day, we, along with some of our cohorts, got a call that the New York Police Department wanted us to do a floor show for them at their annual dance. We assumed we would be paid—no one in those days would ask the Police Department "how much?"

So we did two performances of the show. One at dinner time and another later in the evening when the officers were dancing and drinking with their wives and sweethearts and having a great time. When the time came for us to be paid we were amazed. Instead of money, they gave us bags about half the size of body bags full of yellow cheese sandwiches.

There were at least 500 sandwiches stacked in about five bags. It was wintertime so we could keep the sandwiches on the windowsill and outside on the fire escape. Everybody who was hungry had another cheese sandwich. By the time spring came and the bread and cheese were all curled up we couldn't look another cheese sandwich in the face. But I'm sure the New York Police Department appreciated our efforts.

Solid Boffo in Nabe Vaud.
  —Billboard *Magazine*

Variety Show Biz Talk

Reporters for *Billboard* and *Variety* magazines really write in a phonetic language all their own. When Ken and I and Charlie Reed were caught by a *Billboard* reporter in two neighborhood theatres we played in Philadelphia, he described us in one line:

The Three Ambassadors are Solid Boffo in Nabe Vaud.

Translation: We were a smash hit in neighborhood vaudeville.

A true professional believes in a second chance.
　　　　　　　　　　　　　—Hal Raymond

"YPSILANTI"

The Warner Brothers studio where Warner made the selected short movies was located at Avenue M, the last stop on the subway way out in Brooklyn. We worked there many times for a director who signaled that the final shooting was a wrap by shouting "Ypsilanti" which could be heard all over the studio. Everything came to a halt, the lights came up and the shooting for that day was over.

An unprecedented spirit prevailed among some professional directors and producers during those depression days. And I think it pertained only to the period of the depression because I did not see evidence of it later on. It was simply that they would not fire anyone unless they really had to and had no other recourse. They were aware as everybody else that jobs were few and far between and very hard to come by, and if it were at all possible, they would keep from firing people. I know. That's what happened to me.

We were shooting a scene with Jack Dempsey, the famous heavyweight champion of the world. He was in the ring sparring with a top flight boxer portraying a professional fight. Ken and I were cast as sportswriters at ringside in the most prominent seats available.

The director shouted "Action!" The shooting lights came on, the fighters started to box, the small camera that focused on the action at ringside started coming around, coming around. I had been out all night the night before.

The heat and the retakes had already taken their toll. I was sound asleep.

When the camera swept the ringside where we were sitting all the other characters were writing and scribbling and shouting as sportswriters did in those days. When the camera focused on me I was sitting there snoring, slumped down in the seat with my press card stuck in my hat band.

Then all hell broke loose.

The director hollered, "Cut!" He came over to me, glared at me about three inches from my face, and shouted, "What the hell's wrong with you! You ruined the whole shot. Do you realize what you have done? We have to throw the whole damn thing away. Everyone has to work overtime [without pay in those days] just because of you!"

I received the greatest dressing down of my life at the time.

But he did not fire me. He knew me very well from times I had worked for him in the past. He just dressed me down. Dempsey climbed down from the ring, his sparring partner sat in the corner, everyone else broke ranks for five minutes. Then we got up, the actors took their places, and we did the whole thing over again. This time it was shot successfully and I made damn sure I was awake.

Despite all the trouble I caused that particular director he forgave me by calling me back for work time and time again, especially when he called for "highly experienced" dancers. Whenever he saw me standing among scores of people who wanted to be picked for a particular short subject he would pick me every time.

Selected short subjects usually followed a pattern. The feature picture would end, then the news of the day would be projected—Warner Brothers News of the Day or Fox Movietone News—and they would be followed by the selected short subjects. These were tightly produced, highly budgeted, short movies running from 10 to 15 minutes in length. After one or two of the selected short subjects were shown, the orchestra would start to play. It would rise up to stage level from below the seating level on a huge elevator and the live stage show would begin. It took practically all day to go to the movies. And in the days before universal air conditioning the theatres that provided it were cool havens against summer heat.

The selected short subjects were showcases for established performers and were often the avenue for new comers to break into the business. We appeared with many top performers such as Hal LeRoy and Mitzi Mayfair who were sponsored by Ziegfield.

Some of the finest dancing I had ever seen took place when we had intermissions called "costume breaks." We couldn't sit down because we would wrinkle our full dress suits, so we leaned back against tilted "lean-away" boards and watched and danced spontaneously. It was wonderful.

If the director or producer knew you were a good, reliable performer, he would be extremely patient and do anything to keep from firing you. A case in point was a selected short subject about Ireland. The lead singer was supposed to begin with the song: "Has Anyone Here Seen Kelly, Kelly from the Emerald Isles?" He tried to sing that line. It must have been twenty times and he could never get it right. The poor guy was sweating blood even though he was a seasoned performer. He became very nervous and the more nervous he got the more he flubbed the line. He didn't want to be fired, he needed the job badly. Eventually the producer calmed him down and babied him until he finally did it right and the scene was shot. That lead singer and my sportswriter role were heartwarming evidence that producers and directors would do what they could to keep from firing performers who had proved themselves even though they were having a bad day.

The best and hottest trumpet on the Broadway beat was at the corner of 7th Avenue and 49th Street.

—Hal Raymond

NTG's Paradise Club

Ken and his partner at the time, Roy Paige, were booked for a month at NTG'S Paradise, a club owned by Nils T. Granlund that he operated on the second floor at 49th and 7th Avenue.

As good luck would have it, the star of the show was Bunny Berigan, the great trumpet player who had just formed his own band after playing for many years with Tommy Dorsey and others. He was regarded, certainly, as one of the greatest trumpet players of all time. He recorded a song from the Follies called "I Can't Get Started with You" that became a cult song for him. This song, coupled with his other great hit, "If I had the Wings of an Angel," would start his fans stomping and whistling and shouting. People came from great distances and held tickets far in advance to catch his performances. I was playing at a different club at the time but every chance I got I'd stand backstage with Ken and Roy and listen to Bunny Berigan and marvel at his artistry. It was a thrill just to be there.

Memories are the bridge to yesteryears.
                    —Hal Raymond

Dan Dailey "Just Won't Do"

I would like to say a few words about Dan Dailey the well known movie star. He was an old friend, a one-time dancing partner and a roommate.

Dan would come from his home in Long Island and stay with Ken and me at the Landseer Apartments. I can remember particularly how his feet stuck out at the bottom of the bed—he was a tall man, about six-six.

Dan and I were in love with two girls who were on the road in different shows. He had discovered, with the ingenuity of a young man in love, that special delivery air mail was delivered to the Grand Central Post Office at 4 o'clock in the morning. We would set our clock, wake up and go down to the post office, get our mail, come back and read it, put it in our pockets—we had our inside pockets enlarged so we could keep our letters with us—and go back to sleep. Ken and I wanted to work Dan into our act as a replacement for a partner who had left. We played two break-in dates with him that were caught by Marvin and Irving Yates, the brothers who booked most of the Loews theatres in this part of the East. Later they took us aside and said that Dan Dailey "just wouldn't do. That he couldn't cut the mustard"; that we would have to keep looking for another partner.

We were working at the time in a large production at the Roxy Theatre that was put on by Gay Foster. The now defunct Roxy Theatre—at the corner of 50th and Broadway—was a spectacular showplace and Gay Foster was well known as a fine producer who specialized in staging

38

enormous revues. We had worked with her a number of times in the past.

When we got the word that Dan Dailey "just wouldn't do" and we told him, he cried like a baby. He said, "You and Ken have made good and I'm through." We said, "You're not through, Dan, it's just one of those things." He disappeared for about six weeks and then surfaced again at Ben Marden's Riviera, a big night club in New Jersey, owned by Lou Walters, the father of a famous TV journalist. Dan was seen there by a Hollywood scout. They gave him a screen test and cast him in a picture about Nazism which was beginning to spread around the world. It was called "The Mortal Storm," a very fine picture that had nothing whatsoever to do with dancing. He played the part of a young Nazi officer who was so imbued with the Nazi spirit that he turned in his own mother and father. The movie was nominated for an Oscar. Dan received rave reviews and I had to admit that he was one of the meanest Nazis I had ever seen on the screen.

From then on he was firmly ensconced in Hollywood and appeared in many dancing films with leading ladies such as Betty Grable and others. We used to laugh about when he thought he was through and that we had "made good." A number of years later, Dan appeared at the Oakdale Theatre near New Haven, Connecticut. When I went back to say hello, he saw me, waved over the heads of those around him, came running up, grabbed my hand and said, "Hal, it's been a long time, but nothing has changed."

So I say good-bye to Dan Dailey, a long-time friend, a short-term dancing partner and a roommate who was always a classy gentleman. Ken and I were deeply saddened by his early demise that came many years too soon.

I always believed that a custom-made suit was a good investment.

—Hal Raymond

Getting Married on Stage in Jimmy Walker's Suit

We had come by one of Mayor Jimmy Walker's suits, a beautiful double-breasted pin stripe. It had been given to a partner of ours, Charlie Reader, as a result of doing a political benefit for the Mayor. A benefit was a show we'd be paid for in anything but cash. In this case, it was one of the Mayor's suits.

Jimmy Walker was a good Mayor for New York. He was dashing and debonair, just the man for the World's Fair and the periodic arrivals and departures of the Hindenburg circling over New York to and from its moorings in New Jersey.

Charlie and Ken and I shared Jimmy Walker's suit with two other friends—so any one of the five owners could wear it when an occasion important enough arose. We were all about the same size and weight—I suppose because we all had about the same amount to eat and were trimmed down, in fighting weight. I weighed about 120 pounds.

My fiancee, May Turpin, and I had decided to get married. She was touring in "50 Million Frenchmen" and I was in a musical comedy called "The King's Scandals" at the RKO Theatre in Newark. Some of the dialogue in the show kidded Mayor Jimmy Walker about the 50 or so suits he owned. We all decided that getting married was an important enough occasion so that I could wear Jimmy Walker's suit; it fit me perfectly.

Plans for our wedding took on an unusual aspect. We agreed to be married on the stage of the RKO Theatre after the finale of "The King's Scandals." There was a lot of publicity beforehand and the audience was invited. We had rehearsals for the wedding just as it is traditionally done. The entire cast took part on the night of the actual wedding because we were all in the final scene. The set was the King's courtroom and included a big white throne. The minister sat there alongside one of the headliners, Gil Lamb, a gifted contortionist. As they were received, gifts were described to the audience. I remember I got a new suit—maybe to replace Jimmy Walker's. (I was the first to be married in that suit, but there were others who would wear it at their weddings.) Members of the cast were evenly divided and left the stage going out each side of the stage as though it were a routine in the show.

It was an exciting time. Everyone came up to congratulate us, even people from the audience. There was much laughter and music and hugs and smiling faces. It was an evening never to be forgotten.

May received a gown, a beautiful hat and a blue purse with about 50 bucks in cash which we lost that night. We left the purse in the taxi cab and never got it back. When we got to the hotel and realized the purse was gone I was especially upset. There were four Irish Sweepstakes tickets in it, which was a very big event in those days. It was conducted by the Irish Hospital Fund and the winning tickets were announced on the day it ran its big race, called the Grand National. It was possible to win the undreamed of sum of about $90,000 to $100,000! May regretted losing the beautiful blue purse; I regretted it even more because, who knows, I could have been winning the Irish Sweepstakes with the four lost tickets. We would never know because we had nothing to show for it.

Even though losing the purse, the money and the Irish Sweepstakes tickets made the day end on a somewhat down side, we were very happy. May and I were married for many years and appeared together as a dance and comedy act known as "Hal Raymond Handicapped by May."

Please send a carbon copy—no questions asked.
—Hal Raymond

Did You Ever Play the Palace?

May and Ken and I played the hallowed stomping ground
of every variety performer: The Palace!

The Palace at 47th and Broadway was the magic mecca,
the ultimate, the goal of goals, the summit, the dazzling
height from which you could look out and say your life was
really worth living.

We played there with the Anatole Freidland version of
"50 Million Frenchmen" that had been trimmed down to
unit size, meaning it had gone through legitimate show sta-
tus on Broadway and also on the road. He bought the rights
when it closed on the road and we were in it as a full unit
production with the same title and music.

Although I occasionally received fan mail I didn't usually keep it. But one had me spellbound. Not the content,
but the address. It had my name on it and then underneath
it said:

In care of THE PALACE
New York City, NY

Those words were absolute magic to me. I was
enthralled by the fact that my name and that of the Palace
were on the same envelope. I kept it with me all the time,
changing it from one inside coat pocket to another as I wore
different clothes. It got dog eared and rumpled but I cherished it. I'd take it out every once in a while and read the
magic address to myself.

It was written to me by a young woman who sat in the

second row for every performance. I don't know how she got the same seat all the time or even how she got my name. The letter didn't mean much to me at the time because I thought it was the kind of fluff that performers sometimes receive from people in the audience. She wrote: "You're going to be the next Jimmy Cagney."

I took a lot of kidding from Ken on that score and some raised eyebrows from May. But there was no flirtation intended. She had signed her name, which I have forgotten, but didn't include an address or telephone number. It's the only piece of fan mail I really wanted to save. But it got lost somewhere along the way. The fact that it really existed, however, still gives me a warm, happy glow.

*When in doubt always go to Minsky's and lose that
vague, unfocused feeling.*

—Hal Raymond

Minsky's Burlesque

Turning to folks who made jokes, such as "here he comes
now," and who carried warm air bladders with which to
beat one another and everyone else within reach on the
head, was known as "Minsky's Burlesque," where the "Top
Banana" ruled the runways.

The standard fare of a burlesque show was the strip
dancers who were the best in the world, comedians referred
to as "Top Banana," "Second Banana," etc., good looking
chorus girls, male dancers who often argued with the men
in the audience, and of course, the traditional "Candy
Butchers." "Candy Butchers" went up and down the aisles
selling boxes of candy. If someone in the audience yelled,
"Hey, Charlie. A box of chocolates over here," the candy
would be thrown with unyielding accuracy over the heads
of the others and land precisely at the customer's place.

The main attraction, of course, was the strippers and
the seasoned drummers who caught every sinuous move-
ment of the stripper with rim shots. You'd have to see them
working together to appreciate their true artistry. Among
the best strippers in the world were Margie Hart, Billy
Myers the California Bombshell, Georgia Sothern, Midge
Park, Peaches Strange and others.

There were two shows a day at Minsky's. Every seat
cost $2.50, which was a tremendous sum in those days, and
every seat was taken.

We had a partner one season who was truly a brash native New Yorker. His name was Barney Elmore. He would run down the center runway and beat the patrons on their heads with a warm air bladder. The audience, who couldn't wait to see the strippers, would yell, "Get off the stage, you bum! Get lost!" But he would keep running up and down, yelling at the audience and waving the air bladder until he would finally go off looking back over his shoulder and scowling.

When Margie Hart came out to start her number it was our delightful job to sing two songs behind her: "Margy, I'm always thinking of you, Margy," and "I love you. I love you,"which was a hit song of the day, as she gradually removed what little she had on with her own type of magic. She handed her bra to Ken, her tiny skirt to Barney Elmore, and I was the lucky one, I got what was left, her G string. All the time the audience kept yelling, "Get lost you bums. Get off the stage!" So we would leave the stage and Margie would do her routine which was absolutely fantastic. We were the legitimate act sandwiched in between the comedians and the strippers. I must mention a terrific comedian, Gus Schilling.

It was a mighty cold winter in New York that year and we were extremely lucky to be working at Minsky's for the whole season. Being there even made it possible for us to advance cash occasionally to a few out of work show business friends so they could buy food for the week. Barney Elmore was a true burlesque performer with just the right amount of brashness and good humor to make it work. This was the period when the prospect of war began to loom on the horizon. Barney was eager to join the Air Force and thought he had a better chance of doing so by going to Canada, which he did. We never saw or heard from him again.

The wartime phrase "Kilroy was here" was another way of saying farewell to Barney Elmore.

A marriage of initials that changed our world.
                                        —Hal Raymond

FDR and the NRA

One of the many wonders of the times was initiated in 1933 by President Franklin D. Roosevelt, who realized that if the country were going to recover from the Depression, people had to have enough money to eat and keep working even though they had a job but had to wait for wages to be paid to them.

His brain child, the National Recovery Act, the NRA as it was called, operated under the direction of General Hugh Johnson, authorized the government to establish minimum wages and maximum hours through a series of labor codes that eventually affected more than 22 million Americans. It was of immense benefit to us in the variety theatre. It meant for the first time that performers had to be paid a living wage while they were rehearsing, or at least be paid enough money to buy food and have a place to sleep and not be at the mercy of some producer who could let variety performers fend for themselves or starve until the show opened. It was not uncommon to see performers in big stage shows actually faint during strenuous rehearsals from lack of proper food.

When some producers realized that their absolute dictator role had been abolished and they had to pay performers while they rehearsed in preparation for opening the show, you'd think they had been stabbed in the heart and the wound was fatal. But they survived. We all survived.

So, hooray for the NRA for helping variety show business people who desperately needed it at the time.

Sometimes value increases with time.
                    —Hal Raymond

Henny Youngman Was Worth Three Dollars a Night to Me

Henny Youngman, a tall, thin unknown comedian opened with us at a club in New Jersey and couldn't buy a laugh. He was desperate. He was out there in front of an audience telling jokes that had just enough dialogue to reach the punch line as quickly as possible, which was the objective of this new type of comedy at this time. But he was met with absolute stony silence all around.

Finally he came over and said to me in a whisper, "Hal, stand there, you and May, and get other people to laugh."

I said, "Henny, I know you're laying a big one out there, but things will get better."

He said, "Just laugh at the punch lines."

So I said, "O.K." Every time he told a joke we would laugh it up. It didn't work out as well as he thought because he wasn't what you would call a smash hit. He barely got to come back the next night, when the original engagement was for three nights. But Henny Youngman was very important to me. He meant three dollars a night because I was the only one with a car. I got three dollars round trip for driving him back and forth from the corner of 46th and Broadway and by ferry to the club in New Jersey. I wanted him to be held over very badly. He got a little better toward the end; and we became more hip to the places we should laugh. We laughed, not too loudly, but enough to help build him up.

The entertainers who also paid three dollars round trip included, in addition to Henny Youngman, two strippers and an old juggler who had been around for a long time. The girls complained about sitting next to him. I remember saying to them, "Some day you'll be old, too, and you'll be glad to sit next to anyone." I had a black 6-cylinder six passenger Pontiac Silver Streak with the much vaunted and highly advertised cat walk cooling radiator grill which was the idol of young entertainers and made me look like I was worth a million bucks.

As audiences became more accustomed to his style of one-liner comedy, Henny Youngman began to make his mark at Las Vegas and on the West Coast and came to be regarded as the epitome of wit and humor in his field. And deservedly so.

Love is thicker than hard times.
—Hal Raymond

Aunt Kate

Aunt Kate was an unusual woman. She was a gifted corporate secretary so she always had good jobs. But she had one curious compulsion. Every so often she would put an ad in the paper, sell her furniture and move to a different apartment. She did this, it seemed, constantly. During the time we were there, she moved at least a dozen times, or so it seemed.

One early spring, May and I were staying with her for a few days while we waited for new costumes to be finished. After dinner we played a game that is now considered a child's pastime, but then it was a new fad sweeping the country. Everybody played it. It was called "Pick Up Sticks." We finally went to bed. We had been there a couple of hours when Aunt Kate came in and woke us up, and said, "Get up."

We asked, "Why?"

She said, "I just sold the bed. I'm moving and I'm getting all new furniture. You can sleep on the overstuffed chairs in the living room."

We dragged sheets and blankets into the living room and settled down as comfortably as we could. A few hours later she shook us both awake and said, "Get up. I just sold the chairs." This sounds like a comedy routine but it is the God's truth.

She said, "I intend to sell everything so you might just as well put the sheets and blankets on the rug and sleep there right now." Which we did. This kept up all night as she sold item after item. When we woke up in the morning,

51

stiff and sore from sleeping on the floor, the apartment was practically empty.

Aunt Kate was a tall, pretty blonde who had a very stately manner. She moved into and out of apartments directing the moving men with the ease and composure of a dowager overseeing her country estate. But we didn't care. We loved her, we loved her great sense of humor and her wonderful cooking. Sometimes the sweetest words we could possibly hear were, "And don't be late."

May and Hal Raymond toast their marriage after their wedding ceremony on the stage of "The King's Scandals" in Newark, New Jersey.

A trio grows in Brooklyn—Gladys, Hal and May.

Hal Raymond solos at "The Bowery" in Detroit—look at that tie. It's really tied to stay.

May and Hal in his gray doeskin tail suit swinging along at the El Dumpo.

Montage of Hal and May Raymond knocking them out at the El Dumpo.

Ken Paige, Hal Raymond's brother—one of the truly handsome men in the variety theatre—between coughs at the El Dumpo.

Bookmaker betting scene at Longchamps racetrack in "50 Million Frenchmen"—trying to win a buck for every Frenchman; May Raymond at extreme right.

Finale of "50 Million Frenchmen" and the birth of the hit song, "You Do Something to Me."

Hal, May and Gladys—from here we can see Hollywood from the Mar-Jo.

This lobby photo of Gladys, Hal, and May caused a lot of pushing and shoving to get in line to get tickets.

The dude on the right is the letter-getter, Hal, performing at the Palace with Ken. The snapshot was taken by Dan Dailey from a seat in the second row.

Ken and Roy Paige at the Palace. Again, Ken is the dude in the double-breasted jacket.

Gladys, Hal and May invoking all the help they can get at the end of their new international rhythm number at Jimmy Kelly's.

Hal plays backup to their little dog, Tempo, on the Brooklyn subway coming home from the Woodside and still jumping. May is enchanted and immobilized by the beauty and breadth of his tone. ("Maybe he'll hit the right tone next time.")

Little Tempo hitting and holding a high C to cap her performance.

May and Hal Raymond dance for the Maxwell House Coffee advertising campaign: "A strenuous life, this dancing."

May and Hal Raymond dance for the Maxwell House Coffee advertising campaign: "Hey, Mom. Look at me."

This Maxwell House Coffee advertisement—appearing in the June 12, 1937 issue of the Saturday Evening Post—is an example of the advertisement appearing in major publications for months which featured Hal and May along with other popular headliners.

In spite of his famous 100-mile-an-hour fastball, this is the group that brought a look of terror to Satchel Paige's eyes. Jimmy Kelly's ferocious team included: table singers, Hal Raymond, the dancing first baseman (holding the glove), the men's superintendent of sanitation services, the maître d', two busboys, an Irish tenor, a publicity man, team manager and assorted backup players.

STARTING YOUNG

37 YEARS AGO A FIGHT MANAGER RAN INTO JIMMY KELLY ON THE STREET AND SAID, "COME ON KID, WE'VE GOT A FIGHT TONIGHT." SO JIMMY, BARELY PAST 14 YEARS WENT UP TO STAMFORD, CONN., AND FOUGHT TOUGH JOHNNY HINES TO A DRAW IN HIS FIRST "PRO" FIGHT.

Jimmy **Kelly**

FROM 1900 TO 1905 HE BEAT THE BEST OF THEM. AMONG THE FAMOUS MEN THAT FELT THE POWER OF HIS FISTS WERE: TOMMY FELTS, JIM GARDNER, JOE TIPMAN, GEO. MCFADDEN.

JIMMY HAD TO STAND UP BETWEEN THE ROUNDS OF ONE OF HIS MOST IMPORTANT FIGHTS TO KEEP A BROKEN RIB FROM STICKING THROUGH THE FLESH — HE WON THE FIGHT.

"KID" CHOCOLATE THE ONLY FIGHTER TO TURN "PRO" EARLIER THAN KELLY. THE "KEED" STARTED AT 12!

LATER HE TURNED MANAGER AND HANDLED SOME OF THE BEST, AMONG THEM WERE **STANLEY KETCHEL** AND **JACK BRITTON** — BUT HE HAD TO LET JACK GO BECAUSE HE COULDN'T GET HIM ANY FIGHTS... ...HE WAS TOO CLEVER. KELLY NOW HOLDS THE DISTINCTION OF BEING THE OLDEST CABARET OWNER IN NEW YORK!

JIMMY ONCE EMPLOYED **IRVING BERLIN** AS A SINGING WAITER

Montage of Jimmy Kelly's background.

"Cyrano de Durante" autographs a photo for Hal and May.

The times are deadly; this place is dangerous.
                              —Shakespeare

Double Trouble

In those days "doubling" was known as working two different club dates on the same evening by driving and parking close enough to the second club in time to do that show and get back to the original club to do the late show.

Once again those good-hearted and understanding Louisville detectives helped us out. They gave us permission to park our car in the middle of a long alley and let it stay there while we were doing our show at the second club and then driving back to our original engagement. The pre-war scene in Louisville was a mix of armed forces as security against espionage at Fort Knox and the usual riff-raff that was drawn to pre-war bustle in the big cities. An example of the worst element were three truly rotten characters who a short time before had assaulted and beat up a military policeman. They had even gone so far as to steal his .45 calibre sidearm. And believe it or not, they were out on bail!

They made themselves thoroughly obnoxious by standing along the narrowest ramp where the show girls had to make their entrance and exits, and as a result the girls were almost forced to rub up against them. These low lifes became aware that May and I and a beautiful show girl left the club at the same time every night to dash to our car and drive to our second club date. Invariably, they'd stand in our way and follow us part of the way out of the door, acting in an insolent and insulting manner. One night they kept following us and as we headed into the long alley to reach our car they ran up and kept walking about 15 feet behind us. I told the girls that it looked like we might have to make a run for it and for them to run as best they could in their high heels.

"When we get to the car," I said, "don't grab my arm."

I was armed with a snub-nosed 2-inch barrel Colt detective .38 special revolver in the inside pocket of my dress coat. If worse came to worst I thought I could hold them at bay until we all got to the car and locked the doors.

We all knew, without saying it, that rape and perhaps even more was on their minds.

As we ran down the long alley, I realized we were going to be caught before we ever made the car. So I said to the girls, "Stop; turn around and stay behind me. Don't grab my arm." So we stopped immediately, turned around and faced them. Apparently we took them by surprise. They stopped, too, and started to saunter towards us in an insolent, leering manner. The ringleader was the one in the middle. I stared at him and he stared back and I knew the time had come for some sort of action. Without saying a word, I stood in front of the girls, put my hand inside my coat pocket, and grasped the butt of the revolver in a way that could not be mistaken. This stopped the leader cold in his tracks. The other two hung back behind him. I stared at him for what must have been at least a full minute without uttering a word, but in a manner that made him realize that if he kept coming towards us he was going to get shot. Thanks to the good Lord who was watching out for us, the ringleader made a surly remark, turned and started walking back the way he had come. The others followed him.

We got in our car and, shaking all the way, drove to our second club date. When we had finished, we drove back to our regular club. As we went in, we asked the detectives who were on duty at their regular table if we could leave our car in front of the club. The lieutenant in command asked why, so I told him the whole story while the other detectives listened. He said to me, "Don't worry, Hal. Of course you can park in front of the club. The only thing you did wrong was that you didn't shoot the bastards."

There is never really an excuse for walking to work.
—Hal Raymond

How to Finance a Car—
Depression Style

A few years down the road the Great Depression still had
us in its grip.

We were in Louisville when we had a particular run of
bad luck and didn't know what to do. Some of our
wardrobe had been stolen and we would have to go back to
New York to replace it because we couldn't get what we
needed in Louisville. Our music had also been stolen. We
were in a real downspin and to make matters worse the last
payment was due on our very high-flying car for the times,
our black Pontiac 6 cylinder 1933 model. We were afraid
we'd be stranded if our car was repossessed. In desperation
we stopped at a Pontiac dealer and said, "What can we do?
Will you give us a break and abate this last car payment
that's due?"

He said, "No. But there is one thing you can do. Buy a
new car."

We said, "How can we buy a new car when we can't
pay for the old one?"

He said, "If you buy a new car, you can get 45 days
from the day of possession to make your first payment and
you'll be straightened out by then."

I said, "That's a wonderful idea." May and I talked it
over and decided to trade in our car as the down payment
on a new cherry-red Straight 8 Silver Streak 6-passenger
Pontiac still with the much vaunted and highly advertised
catwalk cooling radiator grill. The absolute latest model.
Altogether with the grace period of about two months to

make our first payment we were sure we'd be back on our feet by then. In the meantime, we would travel in style.

The point I'm making is that if you were in a bind during the Depression but still retained confidence and faith in the indomitable spirit of the American people there was always a solution.

A genius finds himself.
—Hal Raymond

Red Skelton Calls It Quits

I'd like to talk about a great entertainer and his almost early exit from the variety theatre which would have been a national crime against millions of Americans who loved and followed him. It has to do with Red Skelton and two nightclubs in Montreal situated in a single building at the corner of St. Catherine's and North High Street, one of the main crossroads in Montreal. The club on the first floor was known as the "Tic Toc"; the club on the second floor was called "The Stanley Grill."

Ken, and his partner at the time, Roy Paige, were booked at the Tic Toc along with Red Skelton. Red was feeling low. The only work he had been able to get previously was as an MC at dance marathons which were very popular across the country. May and I were performing at the Stanley Grill on the second floor. Red often talked about how discouraged he was and how he hoped that the new routines he was working on would change his luck at the Tic Toc Club. He said that if he couldn't make it at the Tic Toc he was going to leave show business for good.

But luckily his luck did hold out. Red became a smash hit at the Tic Toc after he really got started. Finally Ken and Roy's month-long engagement was finished, and May and I finished our gig and left for another engagement, but Red Skelton was there for nearly a year. As it turned out, Red Skelton became a national treasure on radio and TV after he went to the West Coast and Hollywood. His routines, including "Clem Kaddiddlehopper" and the punch drunk prize fighter called "Cauliflower McPugg" who would hear airplanes and birds coming over and who was always ducking imaginary objects hurled at his head, saying "They're coming over"—became entertainment classics. So, instead of leaving, Red Skelton became part of American folklore. It was a real honor to have worked with him.

So we say, "Great work, Red. Everybody was glad that you didn't quit. Good-bye to Clem Kaddiddlehopper and 'look out; they're coming over.' "

See you around.

*　　*　　*

Dear Red:

We all realized at your passing on September 17, 1997, that no matter how many years have passed since our initial contact—when we were young and full of hope and dreams—and when we contemplate the sad events of the recent past, we rationalize they could always use a real clown up there to a far greater advantage for everyone forever. So we close this little tribute to you by not saying good-bye, but so-long, Red. Not forever but just for now. See you around.

—Hal Raymond

Sometimes the road to a safe haven can be difficult.
                                                —Hal Raymond

Midwinter Drive

It was wintertime, sometime in February when we had to leave Montreal because we had been booked into "Palumbo's" in Philadelphia. This was a famous Italian dinner theatre that produced excellent shows and had the best Italian food imaginable. It was run by an extremely popular young man, Frankie Palumbo, a member of the family that had owned the dinner theatre for years.

We took our new cherry-red Pontiac Straight 8 out of the state garage where it had been impounded all the time we were in Canada because we weren't allowed to drive it without a Canadian license and insurance. When we got in the car and started out on a 500-mile trip to Philadelphia I hadn't driven for nearly a year and had practically forgotten how to and had to teach myself all over again. To make matters worse, a heavy snowstorm began. We were driving in sheets of snow, just crawling along, peering through blackness and trying to keep from sliding off the highway. Despite the fact that we were in the middle of a storm with snow swirling around us, it still seemed quiet and peaceful. Almost too peaceful.

All of a sudden there was a terrific commotion. Lights went on. Sirens went off. What had been a snowy, empty highway turned into a brightly lighted stretch of road with two buildings on each side. We had accidentally driven through customs barriers. The guards, who were usually convivial and friendly, were menacingly suspicious. I think they were a little frightened themselves and had probably assumed no one would be coming through at that time of night and in that kind of weather. They made us open the trunk of the car, take out every suitcase, open it up, spread out all the contents and questioned us repeatedly about what we had to declare. We kept saying we had nothing to declare, that we were a couple of show people who had to get to Philadelphia in time to rehearse our act and appear in the next evening's show. After much searching and questioning, they finally let us go on. And we did get to Philadelphia, despite the guards and the bad weather, in time to open at Palumbo's dinner theatre.

The next morning we went out to the parking lot Frankie had reserved for us and were horrified to find that the extra fancy hubcaps on our cherished new cherry-red Pontiac Straight 8 with its newly introduced catwalk cooling radiator grill were gone. The wheels were naked with bare lug nuts sticking out. We were very downcast and told Frankie about it.

He said, "Don't worry, Hal. Let me handle the whole thing."

So the next day when we went out to look at our prized possession all of the hubcaps had been restored to their proper places and were shined and polished. This was the sort of thing Frankie Palumbo would do. He was a kind and complex man who managed a complicated dinner theatre with expert chefs, a huge restaurant, and he booked and reviewed all of the shows to be sure they met his high standards. With all of this he was soft spoken and courteous. Although I never knew anything otherwise, it was rumored he had another side to his personality, one that was interested in prizefighting and the sometimes brutal aspects of it and the heavy betting that often took place as the fight progressed round after round.

So Frankie's act of kindness in taking the time to worry about the hubcaps on our car in the midst of his heavy schedule shows the extent to which this refined young gentleman covered the intense fire and leadership qualities of friendship burning within him. His demise several years later was mourned deeply and affected a great many people.

It wasn't the French Foreign Legion, but it was mighty wild for one night.

—Hal Raymond

"50 Million Frenchmen"

When Cole Porter's earliest big show hit the road it had been a huge success in New York. Its title was "50 Million Frenchmen," with the subtitle: "Can't be Wrong." We were all—Ken, May and I—in the road company of this great production when it opened at the Shubert Theatre in New Haven, Connecticut. One of the featured stars was a beautiful young singer known as Lyn Dore (pronounced Do-Ray). She was billed, in the expression of the day, as the one and only "Hotsie-Totsie."

The unusual part about this opening night is that she had to defeat Yale in one performance. She was on the stage in a white sheath gown and in a surprise pink spotlight that made her appear fantastically glamourous. She was singing a hit song of the times considered the epitome of the blues, "Minnie the Moocher," Cab Calloway's famous rendition of a lady in love. She was holding the audience in the palm of her hand singing "Edie Was a Lady," a sequel to "Minnie the Moocher." The lighting plot kept a diminishing surprise pink spotlight on her décolleté. The effect was so stirring because the song was so good and she did it so well and looked so absolutely ravishing that a strange thing happened. First, however, a little explanation.

This was a Saturday night. Yale had played football that afternoon. As a consequence of the game, a crowd of football players was at the show. They were huge, handsome young men. They became so excited and stimulated by Hotsie-Totsie's performance they started to go up on the stage by steps at each side of the apron. The stage hands became thoroughly alarmed, and to say the least, so was Hotsie-Totsie as she was approached by this mass of male humanity leering and laughing and reaching. The stage hands grabbed belaying pins used for tying up the scenery to handle whatever might happen. We young hoofers got the hell out of the way. They were just too big. Hotsie-Totsie finally got to finish her number, but it was known ever afterwards that Yale and its opponent might play to a tie, but Hotsie-Totsie could defeat them both at the same time.

Hotsie-Totsie had very strong connections with powerful people in New York who were known to the sporting world and the police. They were a very forceful influence. She was the girlfriend of one of the main figures. However, she became fond of Ken, who was a handsome son-of-a-gun and he had a special appeal: he coughed. Whenever he was after someone he had a particular cough that women loved. They felt compelled to hold his head in their arms and make him feel better. He employed it constantly. In the privacy of our dressing rooms we used to kid the pants off him, saying, "If everything else fails, Ken will cough and he'll end up in her arms."

It must be remembered that Hotsie-Totsie had powerful connections in New York. After we finished our run at the Shubert in New Haven we moved to the Shubert in Newark for a two-week engagement. It was a smash hit, as usual.

On the opening day, a telegram arrived at the stage door. I remember it distinctly because it was unique and ominous. Addressed to both Ken and Hotsie-Totsie, the telegram read: "Life and love are very sweet but death is more sincere." It was signed "The boys in New York." That's all. Of course the Newark police knew who the boys in New York were, and we had strong suspicions. But no names were spoken and nothing was said. However, the Newark police department supplied Ken and Hotsie-Totsie with a squad of four men as bodyguards for the two weeks we were there. I guess they were glad when we got out of there and we were too. There was a long jump coming up and Hotsie-Totsie, maybe under pressure from her New York connections, decided to leave the show and was no longer on the road with us.

In one month Hotsie-Totsie had defeated Yale and its opponent and had a police escort while she was in the city of Newark. She was the Marilyn Monroe of her day and when she sang she deserved the adulation she got because she was a sex symbol far beyond the times. I heard later that she was happily married and I hope that's true. So we said good-bye to Hotsie-Totsie and continued on the road with "50 Million Frenchmen." This was a Cole Porter production and everyone knew how fastidious, talented and demanding Cole Porter was about his work. It was a wonderful show, a full musical comedy in every sense of the word. It had its own score and very big hit songs you still hear today. In fact there were two of them. One was "You do something to me, something that simply mystifies me." It was the last song of the show and the public gobbled it up. The other song was a swing song called "You've Got That Thing," which didn't last as long on the charts as "You Do Something to Me," but the show was first-rate. It had a story line and a big beautiful cast. When Cole Porter put on a show he had the taste, the ability, and, what's more important, he had the money to do it right. His shows were, and still are, regarded as jewels of their day.

Although Ken may have used his cough to make himself irresistible, to those who caught his eye, maybe even Hotsie-Totsie, I think he was helped by wearing my new homburg hat that made him look especially dashing. He claimed my hat as his own because he knew I had left it at the cleaners. That hat was dear to me. But he got it out and said to me, "Well, I paid for getting it out of the cleaners. You weren't wearing it so now it belongs to me." So even deep brotherly love can be jarred by a clean, elegant homburg hat.

Sometimes the truth is just as accurate in reverse.
                                    —Hal Raymond

El Dumpo

May and I played at a sophisticated club in Chicago curiously named "El Dumpo," an advertising gimmick, no doubt, proving that "what's in a name" doesn't always pertain to what's behind it.

It was truly unique because it maintained a resident chorus line of six gorgeous show girls, which gave the reverse name "El Dumpo" an even more humorous appeal.

I noticed, after the shows were over and the crowd had begun dancing, that a singular figure would be sitting at the bar alone. He was there practically every night. As was the custom after the shows, performers often sat and talked with patrons at their tables to add a little more glamour to the evening. So, after I had changed from my full dress tail suit and was back in street clothes, I began a conversation with this solitary figure. He was very friendly. We talked for quite a while until I realized, in amazement, that he was Red Grange. I never did know why he was there by himself.

At one time, Red Grange's name alone would draw 60,000 to 70,000 people to the stadium just because he would be there in uniform playing football as a running back for the University of Illinois. He was called the "Galloping Ghost" because he was never in the spot where the opposing players dove to tackle him; instead they would get an armful of his great running guard, Earl Britton, who ran interference for him. Red Grange was also known as "Old Number 77." In those days running backs wore numbers different from the lower even numbers they wear today.

I was flattered that Red Grange, who was now at the peak of his professional career and was still known as the All American Man from his collegiate days, would spend time talking with me. One thing led to another and he found out I also had a sporting turn of mind and was very much interested in great athletes, including race horses. On two different occasions he gave me his selections on horses running at the Old Sportsmen's Park or at Narragansett. One time the horse who was running the following week at Narragansett was named "Housework." In the meantime, May and I had gone back to Cincinnati to see my folks. I persuaded my mother to bet 50 cents with me as part of a $2 bet on "Housework." She was scandalized by the idea of gambling, so we had to keep it confidential. "Housework" ran and he won at 32–1. When we got back to El Dumpo from Cincinnati, Red Grange gave me another selection on a horse named "Hurry Home Harry." When "Hurry Home Harry" ran, he finished first at very healthy odds. I can't quite remember what they were but I know they were in double figures.

Despite the negative aspect of its name, "El Dumpo," we had a wonderful two month run there. I not only had the chance to meet and be with Red Grange occasionally, I also took part in what we would call "innocent wickedness," a far cry from what we experience in show business today. It had to do with dressing rooms for six ravishing, statuesque show girls. Dressing rooms for costumes, the wardrobe mistress and all the backstage paraphernalia that is part of nightclub entertainment, requires considerable space. That was in short demand at the El Dumpo. There wasn't enough room for May and her quick costume changes in one small section and the chorus girls would have had to give up their space to make room for me. So, in a spirit of good-natured fun, they said to me, "Let's all dress together."

And that's what we did! For the weeks we were there, I dressed with the show girls. We had many laughs, got along together and had a lot of fun. Compared to today, they radiated a sense of innocent decency.

When our booking ended and we had to go to another club, they gave me a little party and said, "Hal, we have a couple of presents for you." Each girl gave me a make-up towel of a certain size we all used and they pooled together and got me a new jock strap with a six-inch waist band.

It separates the world—not by millions of miles but by a three-inch-thick oaken door. Like the Welcome Nugget, it has never been replaced.

—Hal Raymond

Jimmy Kelly's—Our Home for Two Years

One night when May and I were appearing at the Swing Club in New Jersey, we met a woman who would have a tremendous impact on our lives. She was Claire Osgood, the managing director for the nightclub, Jimmy Kelly's. She saw us do our act and called me over to her table and asked me if we'd like to work at Jimmy Kelly's. I was so ignorant, I didn't know much about it, but I said, "Sure. We'd like that very much." Little did we know what she was offering us.

So, a date was set for our opening at Jimmy Kelly's. I remember it was on the eighth of January, 1936, on a very cold blustery night in New York City. We were glad to get to the stage door because it was so miserable out. The wind was howling and the street was deserted. When we opened that door we stepped into a world I didn't know existed. The place was really packed and jumping with good humored people having a lot of fun with good food, good music; the band was playing "The music goes down and around and comes out here."

We were overwhelmed by the thought of such a place on such a cold and barren street in such barren times. It was indescribable to step in there and realize that only a three-inch-thick oaken door separated this glamourous existence from the cold outside world. It was a watershed for us and changed our lives completely for the better.

Jimmy Kelly's was located at 181 Sullivan Street in the heart of Greenwich Village in the old Italian section. It was known as "The Montmarte of New York," a title Ed Sullivan, the journalist and drama critic, had given it and which contributed greatly to its success.

Jimmy Kelly was born a poor Italian boy in New York City and did all the things that a poor Italian boy would do to get ahead. But he had a particular sense of fairness, and although he lived through dangerous times and had ties to the high-rolling sporting element of New York, he was known as a man who never carried a gun, unlike so many mobsters in those days. Whenever a difficult situation arose, he used his fists. Eventually he boxed for the middleweight title of the world. He didn't win, but he was established in the sporting world as a handy guy to have around.

The club was started by Jimmy Kelly and a racehorse called "Wedgewood." Jimmy Kelly went up one side of the betting enclosure at the Belmont Race Track and his friend, Pepy, went up the other, each betting $1,000 on the horse Wedgewood to win. They didn't give cash. They gave their markers because the bookmakers knew their markers would be good for the money if they lost. No one ever asked how they would get the money but the money would always be there.

When Wedgewood came in first it was reported that Jimmy Kelly won $50,000. He used the money to start his club. As far as I know, it is the only club that opened on the back of a real long shot and a fast racehorse.

On the opening night, Wedgewood was brought in, given a carrot and had his picture taken standing at the bar. His photo was in the lavish program you could buy from the cigarette girl who, with tips and working in that highly charged atmosphere, held one of the most sought after jobs at the club.

Jimmy Kelly's consisted of two glamourous rooms on the first and second floors of a handsomely refurbished, canopied building which made it unusual for the times. With the uniformed doorman, Charlie, and the canopied entrance, those who pulled up in a cab or limousine knew they were going out and into a world of high style and heavy money. As you arrived, you would be met by Mario who stood by the red velvet rope across the entry way. If you got past him, you were in. Patrons had to be recognized by Mario, or he'd have to decide whether you could get in. He was a wonderfully smooth operator, the smoothest I had ever seen in any nightclub or dinner club.

The first floor was called the Mirror Room. The walls were completely covered with blue mirrors which made it seem twice as big as it actually was. The bar was the smallest half-circular bar I had ever seen. It was also the richest. When you stood at this bar you felt as though you were knee deep in money. The first time I went to it I was amazed. The cheapest drink, a half pint of imported beer, cost $1.50, an unheard of price in those days. The price of champagne was determined by the quality and apparent affluence of the party ordering it, according to the insight and feeling of conviviality of the bartender. Murphy was his name.

Once you were seated, elegant menus gave you a choice of incomparable food prepared by Solly, the Chef, who every night worked his particular kind of culinary magic and brought in patrons in droves.

The Mirror Room had its own band led by an old timer everyone called "Joe." A short flight up was the glamourous Cherry Blossom Room with a band led by a handsome young Italian. He had a wonderful piano player, Lionel Rand, who wrote two hit songs while he was there. One was "Blue Rain"; the other was "I Get the Blues When It Rains." The Cherry Blossom Room, like the Mirror Room downstairs, was small, and being small it created a sense of conviviality. I had never seen so many influential people or so much money packed into a small room before or since.

Celebrities and high public officials were constant patrons at Jimmy Kelly's and they could count on the club's sense of discretion. No one ever mentioned being seen when it was an inappropriate situation. How the tradition got started no one knew. It just happened. And everyone abided by it.

On those occasions when we had to do a special show in the Cherry Blossom Room it was so crowded we could hardly get inside to do our numbers without practically sitting at the patrons' tables.

Our dressing room was a few feet from the entrance to the Cherry Blossom Room. Its door was a paddock door with the name "Wedgewood" embossed on it in the style reminiscent of a Kentucky Derby winner. Ed Sullivan wrote a piece about Wedgewood and the opening of Jimmy Kelly's that gained a lot of attention. When he was coming back to New York from a trip to Paris on the Normandy we all went out to greet him on a tugboat about ten miles out. Man, when we got to the Normandy and looked straight up at it, particularly with the tugboat going up and down, it seemed as though we were looking at a ship about a thousand feet tall.

Walter Winchell was also a strong booster of Jimmy Kelly's. He often gave "orchids to" performers in his column. If you got an "orchids to" you it gave your career a big boost; on the other hand, if he gave "scallions to" someone, it could often cause a career setback. We made Winchell's column with an "Orchids to the Raymonds at Jimmy Kelly's for their new number, 'International Rhythm.' "

In addition to being a man of many talents, Jimmy Kelly had a great sense of humor. We were doing a benefit at the Waldorf Astoria one night that included Duke Ellington and his band playing for the acts as well as his own music. When it came time to do our number, I said, "Gee, Mr. Kelly, I feel I don't belong here. I feel like a pauper. I'm all dressed up in a tail suit and I don't have a quarter."

He said, "Here, Hal. Carry this for me while you do your number, but don't take another doorway out." He handed me five beautiful $10,000 bills. I stuck them in the inside pocket of my full dress suit, and May and I went to do our number. I'm probably the only dancer in the world who did his act with $50,000 in his pocket.

It's really true: you can't hit 'em if you can't see 'em.
—Hal Raymond

Old Satchel Paige Shows His Fastball

A bonafide hardball baseball league had been organized among a few nightclubs in Manhattan including my club, Jimmy Kelly's, Leon and Eddie's, The Village Barn, The Famous Door, and others. We had actually won the championship one year and seeing as how our last show was at 4 o'clock in the morning we were all as sleepy as anyone else when the games were played at about 11 o'clock the same morning.

The New York papers carried a nice little article about Jimmy Kelly's winning the championship and we were very proud. The games were usually played on the diamonds in Central Park. Sports writers would actually come to watch us play and give us notices in their papers. I guess they needed a few laughs.

Apparently someone from the Cotton Club challenged our team for the all-city nightclub championship of Manhattan. Jimmy Kelly, being a sporting man, embraced the idea. So it was written up in the sporting pages about these bleary-eyed nightclub baseball players playing for the all-city nightclub championship of Manhattan. On a beautiful Tuesday morning we all got to Central Park about the same time. To our surprise, Jimmy Kelly was there along with some sports writers and quite a nice little crowd of people. We could see that Jimmy Kelly was visibly disturbed when he was talking to the captain of the Cotton Club team.

I heard him say, "I recognize you guys and I know who you are. There'll be no single lump sum bet on this game but I'm willing to make it about $25 a man even though I see about five Black Yankee players including Old Satch Paige. The rest are Kansas City Monarchs and some others. So I only have one thing to say to you fellas, don't hurt any of my boys. I'll be watching." To my amazement, the other team smilingly agreed.

The game started. It was one, two, three strikes and out in rapid succession for the first three batters. When the Cotton Club players came up to bat they got tired of hitting the ball out of sight—they were leading about 17–0—and the next three guys swung at everything and pretended that a weakly hit ground ball was enough to get them thrown out at first base to end the carnage.

The next inning started with our sterling first baseman batting first. As I came to the plate, I obviously was not hiding my anxiety too well. A big jolly Black catcher laughingly said to me, "Okay, good-lookin'. Don't do anything fancy and you'll be okay. Just stand up there and if you see it, swing at it. Just don't jump around and try to do anything big league and Old Satch will make you look good." So I stood there and swung at what looked like three aspirin tablets hurling down the pike at me about a hundred miles an hour, never deviating from pitch to pitch. After the next batter did the same thing our Columbia University graduate came up to bat. (He had not been able to get a job despite his college degree, and was working at Jimmy Kelly's at what was called our Superintendent of Tonsorial Services.) Much to everybody's surprise, and Satch Paige's dejection, he hit a home run. We all cheered wildly, and nodding approval Jimmy Kelly got back in his limo and left.

The manager took Satch out and called in a monstrous young left-handed relief pitcher who threw the ball, it seemed, even harder than Satch's. For the rest of the game our batters hadn't even finished their swing when you could hear the ball slam into the catcher's mitt. This kept up for the next two and three innings with their constantly hitting the ball out of sight and our side constantly striking out.

With a score of about 47 to 1 and it was now about noon, we all agreed that the game was no longer a true contest of skills and said good-bye to each other.

The report on the sports pages the next day said that our line-up from Jimmy Kelly's consisted, among other things, of two table singers, an Irish tenor, a dancing first basemen, an orchestra leader, and our Columbia graduate slugger. They said we all played valiantly but were no match for the amazingly skilled Cotton Club players. Which goes to show that baseball in America is truly immortal, that baseball players will challenge anybody and that one, two, three strikes you're out will live in our hearts forever.

Proof that it pays to advertise.
—Hal Raymond

Young and Rubicam

One of the best and happiest things that happened to us and that we were unaware of at the time was the professional lifetime benefits of our association with top flight show business personalities in practically every leading publication of the time. It came about when we received a call from one of the largest advertising agencies in New York City, Young and Rubicam. I can still hear the woman's sweet voice who was the account executive handling the Maxwell House Coffee account.

She said, "We would like to photograph you and your partner dancing to use in an advertising promotion we are developing for Maxwell House Coffee."

I said, "We are so busy now, doing three shows a day, early and late, that I just don't think we can do anything else. But thank you very much. We certainly appreciate the offer, but perhaps you can get another dance team."

I can close my eyes and still hear her sweet voice once again saying, "We've looked at every dance team in New York and you are the one we want. You tell us when it will be convenient for you and that's when we will set up our camera crew."

May and I talked it over and I said, "If we could make it some evening around 7 o'clock and be through by 8:30 so we could make the first show at Jimmy Kelly's at 9, I'm sure we could do it." She said she would see what she could do and would call us back. She called the next day and said, "We will make this a special appointment. I'll keep the crew at our studio. We'll meet you here at 7 o'clock. We'll probably shoot for a full hour and you'll be able to make your show at Jimmy Kelly's without any fear of being late."

So we went to Young and Rubicam's studio and they photographed us under lights that were brighter than day. Cameras were going constantly. She said, "You just dance and talk about the steps you are working on, and if you feel the need, instruct each other in them so the atmosphere remains spontaneous." So that's what we did. An hour later, when we were through, she said that in addition to being paid, which was quite a lot in those days, she said she would give us a set of photos which were worth hundreds of dollars more than we would have had to pay for them ourselves. She told us the ad would run continuously in the leading newspapers and magazines of the day and she hoped that it would help us in our career. And she was right. The publicity and exposure changed our lives dramatically and for the good. Our salaries went up and we were constantly called for engagements based on the exposure offered by the advertisement.

Many show business headliners were included in different versions of the ad which ran for many months.

Always shop after 12 A.M. for the best in bloodlines and brains.

—Hal Raymond

"Tempo"

We were coming back from our last show at Jimmy Kelly's about midnight one early spring when we stopped at the Somerset Bar and Grill. A young woman was sitting there. May and I sat down beside her and started talking.

She said, "How would you like a nice little dog?"

I said, "Well I've never thought about it, but I like dogs."

She said, "I have this little puppy, a beautiful little Maltese terrier. Her name is Tempo. I am going to give her to someone who will love and take care of her because the person I was going to give her to is not going to get her."

She reached into her large tote bag and brought up what looked like a ball of white fuzz. It was the Maltese puppy, the tiniest thing we had ever seen. It was about three inches long and a couple inches high. But looking up at us from out of the fuzz was a pair of bright, shiny black eyes that appraised us steadily and calmly. We were captivated on the spot.

We said, "Sure. We'll take her."

We took the puppy upstairs to our room and fixed a bed for her in the closet. We put a little raw hamburger in front of her, tried to make her feel at home and promptly forgot about her until the next morning when we heard a tiny yip and growl. May opened the closet door, bent down and said, "Hey, remember. We have a little dog in here." Tempo had gone in under the shelf for shoes, which was about two inches off the floor, and wouldn't come out. May

101

finally coaxed her out with a little raw hamburger.

We didn't know it then, but Tempo would become a beloved fixture in our lives, giving us nearly 17 years of laughs and companionship. She was truly a remarkable animal, brave and brilliant, easy to train, and sometimes, it seemed to us, she showed more perception about people and events than many of our friends did themselves.

Since she only weighed about five pounds when she was fully grown, it was easy to carry her with us under a big, full-length overcoat or in a deep overcoat pocket. Occasionally we would take her to the movies. She usually sat very still watching the movie with a critical eye. But on one occasion she gave herself away by growling at a Great Dane as he came on the movie screen.

Despite her small size, Tempo had the instincts of a bodyguard and the heart of a lion. She would sleep on the floor next to me and growl and bark if anyone came near. Ken even tried to coax her away from me, but without success. She circled around him yipping and barking until Ken gave up and turned away. Then, satisfied that the danger had passed, Tempo returned to her post by the side of my bed.

She was probably the only dog in the world who would be lowered from a window—sometimes as high as the sixth floor but never higher—when she had to go to the bathroom. She would baffle our friends when she had to go out. Instead of going to the door, she would go to the window and bark. The handy thing about Tempo's willingness to be lowered—I think she really liked it—was that we didn't have to take her out ourselves and walk her like dog owners in the city have to do every day. When she was finished, she would bark and we would haul her back up while we sat in our bathrobes and had coffee and Danish pastries. Being strapped in her little harness and lowered caused some high drama one day when we were staying at the Clifford Hotel in Detroit. The hotel had a courtyard with a 6-foot high fence around it and it seemed safe enough to lower Tempo into it. She was in heat and I was a little worried about her. The manager had assured me, however, that it was okay to lower her down even though a police dog was fenced in next to the courtyard. (Incidentally, we had tried several times to have her bred, but she would have no part of it.) When I let Tempo down, the police dog began to go wild. He knew she was there and I guess she knew he knew she was there. He kept jumping and jumping in his six-foot pen and I thought to myself, "Someday that sucker is going to make that fence."

All of a sudden, he landed on top and scrambled over. I was hauling Tempo up hand over hand as fast as I could as she kept growling. When the police dog got into the yard where Tempo was dangling, he gave a mighty leap, higher I'm sure than Nijinsky ever made, and became the first vertical landing missile in history.

The look of frustration, humiliation and consternation on his face was impossible to describe. As I was hauling on Tempo's rope, he gave one last mighty leap and must have cleared 15 feet, but she was just beyond his reach. On her way up, Tempo passed a man at the second floor window who said, "What the hell is that? A flying dog?"

When I got Tempo safely back in the room, the manager called up and said, "We are running a lunatic asylum. A man just saw a dog fly past his window."

I was amazed at how quickly I could train Tempo, although I had never trained a dog before. She realized she had two names, when I called her "Tiger" she knew that was fun time; when I called her "Tempo" in a different tone of voice she knew it was business time. So when I said, "At ease, Tiger," she would run around and bark like crazy

103

knowing that I was ready to play with her. But when I used a different tone of voice and said "At ease, Tempo," she would sit on her haunches and stay sitting there until I said, "Forward march." Then she'd stand up on her hind legs and keep walking until I said, "Attention."

I think she knew what was coming next, because she would look at me expectantly, and as soon as I said, "Salute," she would put one paw above her eye, and then I would say, "Now we are going to sing."

Which was an absolute riot.

Tempo had a funny little yodeling kind of wail. I had learned how to play, with the help of musician friends, Cab Calloway's opening signature of "Minnie the Moocher" on an old trumpet I had. When I played "hidey-ho"—very badly off-key and scratchy—Tempo, still standing at attention and saluting, would sing along with the trumpet. She could mimic Cab Calloway's refrain perfectly. She would wait until I nodded to her and then she would repeat it. When in a different tone of voice I would say, "Tempo, stop singing and go to your room." She would stop singing and go behind the couch and would not come out until I told her to. The amazing thing about Tempo was that she not only recognized words and performed according to my tone of voice, she could also distinguish what I wanted her to do and how I wanted her to do it. And more amazingly, she had learned all these tricks in about three weeks' time.

A professional dog trainer wanted to buy Tempo, saying he could "do wonders with her." I said, "Fat chance!"

At the time, May and I were booked at the famous swing club in Long Island known as "The Woodside." The song and phrase "Jumpin' at the Woodside" had become synonymous with the times. We appeared with the Hudson De Lange orchestra. Eddie De Lange was the leader. His band and the club were known as one of the "in" spots because Eddie De Lange was a leader in modern swing music.

I was so proud of Tempo I said to myself, "I owe this marvelous little dog something. I'd like to have people see how really clever she is." So one night I decided to take Tempo with me to the Woodside. Later that night when the entire band was in one subway car on our way back to Manhattan, I said, "Fellas, how would you like to hear my little dog sing?"

"Okay," they said. "She's probably better than you are on the trumpet."

I took my trumpet out and played the famous radio signature to Cab Calloway's "Minnie the Moocher." Tempo wailed along with me, but only at the right times. She followed my directions, pointing or nodding at her, as though we were a symphony orchestra.

Tempo did not look like the average Maltese terrier with the usual long hair. She was always coiffed with a puppy cut—never more than an inch or so in length—which made her appear as the perennial puppy. Even though the subway car was rocking and pitching, Tempo never lost her poise, never wavered in her singing. She was a tiny operatic diva for the entire ride. The band couldn't get enough of her. They laughed and clapped and stomped their feet hysterically and made me keep Tempo singing until we got to the station. And Tempo loved every minute of it. By the time May and I got her back to our hotel, she was fast asleep, dreaming of her big break in show business.

The next day, however, she was back at her old job of guarding us and our baggage. She always knew when we were leaving for a new engagement. As soon as we got our suitcases out she would sit patiently by the door until we were all packed and ready to go. The fact that she was called Tempo, the same name that Guy Lombardo put on his four or five speedboats, didn't bother Tempo at all because we all knew she was superior to anything man made. So here's to our wonderful little Tempo in doggy heaven. She deserves to be there.

Clark Gable pulls us through.
　　　　　—Hal Raymond

The Other Side of the Coin

J. Edgar Hoover, Director of the FBI, had just said in the newspapers and on the radio that the most dangerous places in the U.S. were on cross country highways after nightfall.

He was right.

May and I had just ended a number of extremely successful engagements and were feeling pretty prosperous, so we decided to drive home to Cincinnati to visit my folks. Childlike, we wanted to put our best foot forward and show how well we were doing. The expensive new suit I was wearing, May's very fashionable outfit, along with beautiful new luggage, and our flashy cherry-red Straight 8 Pontiac made us look very well-to-do indeed. (As an aside, I had recently seen Clark Gable in one of his early movies called "Night Nurse." He played the part of a small-time gangster who was trying to evade other gangsters who were trying to rub him out. As they were gaining on him in a wild car chase, Clark Gable, as he came over the brow of a hill, in desperation, turned off his lights and skidded behind a closed-for-the night gas station. He kept his motor running. A few seconds later the other car came flashing by and then returned cruising back and forth looking for him. It finally gave up the chase and drove away. I remembered that movie in the next few minutes of real life as it happened to us.)

May and I stopped at an all-night roadside café. I recall remarking to May as we got out of the car that the only other car parked in front of the door was a new Ford V-8, known in those days as the fastest car on the road and a favorite of police as well the highwaymen. There was only one customer in the café when we entered it. He had a tired cup of coffee sitting in front of him. He cased us thoroughly as we came in the door and made us feel very uncomfortable all the time we were there.

I said to May, "If he gets up and leaves at the same time we do we could be in trouble."

And sure enough, as we stood up, paid our bill and headed to the door, he did the same thing just a few steps behind us. We hopped in our car with our little dog, Tempo, waiting to jump into her accustomed seat between us. I stepped on the gas and roared out of there at top speed. I was frightened but not surprised when the Ford V-8 did the same thing and stayed within easy passing range immediately.

When May and I played a club in Louisville we often talked with night squad detectives about the growing number of highway robberies that were taking place across the country. Since they knew we often drove long distances between club dates they explained a technique to help us if we were ever threatened. I frantically thought about it now. They said a would-be robber would probably stay close behind our car for a few miles to frighten us. Then without warning he would probably pass us at high speed, get a short distance ahead and jam on his brakes to force us into a panic stop. Our only recourse, the detectives said, was to do the same thing. As soon as the other car stopped temporarily, we should pass him at high speed without using our brakes.

So that's what I did.

The minute the car passed us and was momentarily stopped, I zoomed around him at top speed and was in front of him by the time he realized what had happened. Then our wild ride began. I was so scared I suddenly became a highly skilled driver and blocked him off at every attempt by staying in front. May was so excited and frightened she turned around, and kneeling on the seat, looked backwards and kept telling me where he was while Tempo stood on her hind legs growling and barking. Panic made me drive recklessly. I even drove through clanging bells and flashing red lights of a railroad crossing. Gradually I built up enough of a lead to look for any means of escape.

And suddenly I remembered Clark Gable and the movie. I made up my mind to do the same thing if any kind of a closed gas station should appear. Luckily one did. I could tell by my high beam headlights that it had a gravel driveway running around in back which made me a masterful driver in the reckless way I was driving. I made the car skid in the right direction as though it were being handled by an expert stunt driver.

I had just gotten behind the gas station and pushed the lights off, with the motor still running, when our nasty new friend came tearing by. He zoomed on past while we sat there shaking. Shortly he came back at a much slower pace, weaving back and forth looking for us. He drove back and forth at least a half dozen times and finally gave up and went back the way we had come.

We pulled out with just our parking lights on and drove as fast as possible until we came to Circleville, Ohio, which we knew would be our next town and pulled into the parking lot of an all-night restaurant. As good luck would have it, we stopped right next to a State Police cruiser. Two state troopers were coming out just as we were going in. One brushed up against our car and said, "Boy you really must have been pushing it. Your radiator and tires are boiling hot!" The radiator didn't worry me, and thank God, due to foresight and proper advice, my car was equipped with Lifeguard tires that had been properly balanced, which removed the danger of blowouts due to excessive heat.

We excitedly blurted out the whole story. The troopers listened intently and to our surprise, accompanied by a little dignified profanity, said, "That sounds like the guy we've been looking for because he always operates that way." They immediately hopped in their cruiser and took off in high speed in the direction from which we had just come.

We got back in our car and shakily drove the rest of the way to Cincinnati. And all the while Clark Cable, unknowingly, had probably saved the lives of two of his fans.

Automobiles could only be born here.
—Hal Raymond

Detroit at Full Speed

Jumping to one of my favorite larger cities, Detroit, where it was possible to offer in a single day such diverse and world class entertainment as the lovely and intimate supper club, the Mar-Jo at Nine Mile Road and Jefferson, the exclusive neighborhood of top level automobile executives; Hamtramik, the populous neighborhood where the Club Bowery could entertain you with the best in show business; and, if you could get up early enough after a night on the town like this, you might get to the ball park in time to hear the home plate umpire at the 1940 World Series holler: "Play Ball."

The Club Mar-Jo opened with great fanfare. We opened with it and had a great run. It was owned, operated and promoted by a very sweet, capable woman. The Club Bowery in the Hamtramik neighborhood was well known for bringing in world class entertainers. We were on the bill with, to my mind, the best storyteller ever to appear at the Bowery, or anywhere else for that matter. His name was Lou Holtz. He was a wizard. He could stay on the stage for hours and people would roar with laughter as he told one story after another. All of his material was refreshingly clean. You could take your whole family and not be embarrassed or offended by off-color jokes or heavy-handed innuendos. He closed his act with what he called the "saddest story ever told."

The gist of it had to do with Lou and three other men

111

who wanted to get to Lou's office on the 33rd floor of his building. The elevators were not running so Lou said, "Well, we'll all tell sad stories as we walk up the stairs. We'll take it real easy and walk up the 33 flights. It won't be so bad." So they started up, feeling vigorous and certain that they could climb the 33 flights easily. As time went on, each one took turns telling sad stories. Time passed. They became exhausted and breathed so heavily they could hardly tell their sad stories. Finally they got to the 33rd floor barely climbing on their hands and knees.

Lou, sitting exhausted on the last step, said, "Gentlemen. I have the saddest story of all. I know we spent an hour walking up here, and now that we have finally made it, I have the saddest story of all. We can't get in. I forgot the key." Although the audience usually had a good idea of what the punch line would be, they waited expectantly for Lou to say it, and when he did, the place exploded with laughter. Lou Holtz was simply a great storyteller. One of the greatest in the variety theatre or elsewhere. I salute him.

The World Series in 1940 was played in Detroit between the Cincinnati Reds and the Detroit Tigers. The bellhop and the room clerk at the hotel where May and I were staying had been riding me all season about how Detroit would murder Cincinnati. We had placed bets with each other and when Detroit lost they were so shattered and had such tears in their eyes that I didn't have the heart to take the money they had lost on their bets.

So, we'll leave as a footnote in the sporting history of Detroit that the Cincinnati Reds took the 1940 World Series from the Detroit Tigers by beating their ace pitcher, Bobo Newson. Bobo added a sad note to this sporting history.

Despite the fact that his father had died early in the series, Bobo went on to win two games, but lost in his effort to win the seventh and deciding game of the series, all the time carrying the sorrow he bore in his heart.

Tail suit days are the happiest days.
      —Hal Raymond

English Doeskin Full Dress Tail Suit

Costumes were an essential part of the variety theatre. They had to be colorful, glamourous, dazzling. That's what the audience came to see. The people in the audience didn't want to see performers in ordinary clothes. They went to the theatre to escape for as long as they could the sheer drabness of their own lives. And beautiful costumes helped them do it.

This was particularly true if you wanted to be known as a class dance act that had arrived. We took special pains to be sure our stage appearance reflected that. Most theatres had "lay back boards" backstage where performers, especially dancers, could lean back against them and rest without mussing their costumes. I had an English doeskin full dress tail suit. Doeskin was an unusual fabric. It was almost like velvet. I happened to have this material available to me because Benny Goodman had ordered a bolt of it from England and had had a tail suit made of it. The tailor told me there was enough material remaining to make me a tail suit if I wanted to buy it, which Benny Goodman didn't know or care about.

(A coincidence: We were on the observation car waving good-bye to our family in Cincinnati when we saw Benny Goodman standing on the observation car of a train next to us going in the opposite direction. He was also waving to friends. As the trains pulled apart, we were waving at each other, and laughing. "Hey," I called out. "You're going the wrong way.")

The tailor, Leeds, was on 46th Street. He knew exactly

what variety show people wanted. I had no trouble getting the doeskin tail suit and others made just the way I wanted them with a little more style than you might see on patrons at the Waldorf Astoria where we worked now and then. I worked exclusively in full dress tail suits at the time. One was of white serge of the finest weight, another had a white Eton jacket for summer wear and the other was a conventional black full dress tail suit.

May usually designed her own costumes when we performed as an act and had them custom made by a dress designer. Of course, costumes were issued to her when she played in the big musicals. Our stage wardrobes were expensive and we took special care of them, packing them carefully in big Hartmann trunks whenever we were on the road.

One night, a young dancer who was just starting out and came every night to catch the show at the Club Mar-Jo, asked me what size my suits were. He said he wore the same size and wanted to buy them.

"But these clothes are ten years old," I told him.

"I don't care," he said. "I'm crazy about them and I know they will fit me."

So I sold him my entire stage wardrobe and from then on I worked in dressy suits known at the time as "lounge suits" or sports coats and slacks. Ken and I kept the suits we had bought at Leighton's at a special sale and which we had rescued from the fire at Mrs. Murphy's rooming house. They had cost $6 and were two-piece double-breasted suits of light blue herringbone weave. We both wore them when we auditioned for the new show being cast by Ed Wynn called the "Laugh Parade." They were beautiful suits and made us feel we were looking our best. Apparently we did because we got the jobs.

(Boys will always be boys) around a Western mainliner.
                                        —Hal Raymond

The Great Train Caper

In our run in "Sons of Fun" we were jumping from San
Francisco all the way to Tucumcari, New Mexico, a long,
long train ride across the old frontier. Our entire company
of "Sons of Fun" occupied two cars on the train. We had
been traveling so long and had so much farther to go we
had done everything we could think of to amuse ourselves.
We played cards, wrote letters, read books, slept, sang, and
even danced up and down both cars.

May and I had our little daughter Carol with us. I
remember the comedian, Joe Besser, dancing with Carol
and he held her high in his arms. She loved it and giggled
all the time. We were bored silly and still had a long way to
go. Then I had a brainstorm of an idea. I had always been
fond of target shooting and carried, in a locked box, a new
Colt revolver model .38 detective special with a 2-inch barrel and a box of 50 cartridges.

Frank, the conductor, had been very friendly. I think he
was as bored as the rest of us. I wondered what would happen if I showed my gun to him and asked if it would be
possible to stop the train—we were out in the middle of
nowhere and were the only train on a single line—so we
could shoot it.

I said, "Is it possible, Frank, to stop the train? It
wouldn't take very long for everyone who wanted to, to
shoot the gun at a target, use the 50 cartridges and get right
back on the train."

Much to my surprise he talked to the engineer, came
back and said, "Okay. On one condition. When I say 'board'

116

you gotta get right back on the train." He said another train would not be coming toward us but would be approaching from behind.

So he stopped the train at a place he thought would be the best. It was a desolate stretch of desert with only cactus sticking up. I went around collecting empty coffee containers and soda cartons and set them up in a row, being careful not to use any glass to shoot at. Everyone lined up to take five shots. Since it was a six-shot revolver I handed it to each one in a safe condition with nothing under the hammer and with five cartridges remaining to follow. I held their hands and arms and kept the gun pointed in a safe direction at the targets. Everyone stood well behind the shooter.

Each person would shoot five cartridges. If anyone hit a target you'd have thought we had a train full of sharpshooters who could shoot like Billy the Kid. They would jump around and howl like crazy. Finally, after about an hour, and the cartridges were exhausted, the conductor said, "Okay. We've got to get back on the train. Now. Now."

He wasn't kidding. We all ran back to the train. The people who were slow we shoved back up and pushed them any way we could because without the little platform step usually on the train at a station it was a high step from the ground. The train was actually moving when Frank got on and waved to the engineer who let out a few loud blasts of the train whistle. We had emptied all the cartridges. Everyone was comparing scores with one another and everyone claimed to be the best shot.

Since I had no more use for the gun and no more cartridges, I sold it to a sporting goods shop in Kansas City. We all toasted the conductor and the engineer for being such good sports. We realized later that they were indeed good sports to stop the train so a bunch of crazy show business people could shoot a box of cartridges out in the desert.

When I think of that actually happening I realize what a furor it would cause today. Every agency in the country would be holding investigations and the media would be interviewing everyone and we'd probably all be in jail awaiting bail. So here's to a sporting conductor and engineer in days that were a little more fun and a little more old-time America. We used the wide open spaces and the revolver as our forefathers did. No one was compromised or the worse for wear and we all had a little fun.

The show can be great—but a mother's love is top banana.
                                        —Hal Raymond

"Sons-of-Fun"

The team of Oley Olson and Chick Johnson was the absolute master of variety theatre comedy. They knew the book from A to Z. Their productions were so good and so all-inclusive it's impossible to praise them adequately without writing a volume the size of a telephone book.

Their musical comedy, "Sons-of-Fun," was the heart and soul of variety comedy and was an informal sequel to their former smash hit, "Hellzapoppin." The road company of "Sons-of-Fun," which was virtually the New York company intact, played at the Shubert Theatre in New Haven, Connecticut. May and I, and our year-old daughter, Carol—who was considered the youngest member of the cast by everyone in the company who adored her—had the good fortune to join it there and go on the road with it for about two years.

May was a gifted entertainer. She did a scene in "Sons-of-Fun" with both Oley Olson and Chick Johnson in the stage box that could be considered a classic example of group dynamics. They began to laugh. All three of them pointed at each other and laughed and bobbed their heads up and down holding their sides. Their laughter was so infectious and so sustained that the audience started laughing with them which, of course, was the basis and thrust of that particular piece of business. Soon they were roaring and rollicking and the audience was roaring and rollicking with them until the scene died the death of exhaustion.

May was one of those beautiful women who was truly

talented. She was blessed with a stage personality that appealed to women who rooted for her as much as the men did.

She deserved an offer given to her by the Screen Actors Guild. In order to join, a new member had to be sponsored by an established movie star. She had sponsors of that calibre, and she could have joined as a "B" player, which meant she could play leads in featured pictures or supporting roles in major productions. Despite being given a chance that most women would have given an arm and a leg for, she refused it. She wanted to take our little daughter back to her home town of New Haven. She didn't think moving around in the variety theatre would be the best atmosphere for her. I agreed and returned to New Haven when the show closed.

*My father always warned me about fast women
but not about slow horses.*

—Hal Raymond

Shot and Shell

When certain elements were brought together in what we called an "intact bill"—which meant the acts would stay together for about four weeks—a very nice atmosphere could be created. This was the case at the Century Theatre in Baltimore. We had to blame "Cyrano de Durante," the "Schnozzola," as the one who was responsible for the harmonious aura that we all lived and worked in during this engagement.

Jimmy Durante was the headliner. We were on the bill as the dancing act, "The Three Ambassadors," Ken and I and our partner, Charlie Reed. A very attractive couple known as "Olive and George" were the second headliners. They were genuine midgets, absolutely beautiful doll-like people, perfect in every way. They had starred in a production called "Tiny Town." The bill also included a marvelous girl singer whose name escapes me.

When all these elements came together with Jimmy Durante among them, it created an extremely happy, congenial feeling. It was impossible to be around Jimmy Durante, especially to watch him onstage four times a day, and remain grumpy.

Right outside the stage door was a small, modern horse room where you could make a wager or two on the horse of your choice. One day I went out the stage door, turned left and went to the horse room. I had a strong hunch that a horse called "Shot and Shell"—no matter what the odds makers held him at, which was about 45–1—would do very

121

well in this one race. I was in the horse room and put my money down on "Shot and Shell," two dollars, which was a lot of money to me in those days. The door opened and in came Jimmy Durante. He said, "Hi, kid. I'm glad to see you here. What do you like in the next race?"

I said, "I've already bet, Mr. Durante, on 'Shot and Shell.' "

He said to me, "Please, kid, don't waste your money on that mule. He won't even come in the money."

"Oh, I feel strongly about him, Mr. Durante. I think he'll win."

He said, "Take your money off that horse and put it on another one."

I liked him and didn't want him to think I'd argue with him so I changed my bet on "Shot and Shell" to his horse. I think this was at Pimlico, the local track.

As horse racing lore has it: "The flag is up. . . . They're off and running . . . "

All the horses were getting called. "Love Me Now" by two lengths. . . . "Miss Lovable" by four. . . . Everybody got a call but "Shot and Shell."

"See, kid," said Jimmy Durante. "I told you; he's nowhere in sight."

As the race progressed we had another call or two. All of a sudden "Shot and Shell" got a call and he was running third. We were all very excited. Horse rooms were dramatic in those days because we could hear the live call from the track on the radio. As they entered the stretch, "Shot and Shell" really turned it on and won going away by a length and a half and paid over $90!

"Gee, kid," Jimmy Durante said to me. "I'm sorry. I'll make it up to you. I'll tell you what I'll do. I'll take your dog to dinner tonight."

A few days later, Ken and I were standing in the wings

watching Jimmy Durante do his act, which we did every day. Suddenly someone pushed between us and put his arms about both our necks. When I turned to see who it was, I was startled to realize it was John Barrymore. His features were so sharp and well defined it was impossible not to stare at him.

"Well, boys," he said to us. "I've been watching you out there. I know you really love your work because you do it so well. And I know it is hard work. Do you really enjoy it?"

We said, "Oh, we really love it, Mr. Barrymore. We really do."

He said he'd see more of us during the week and that he was going to be around a while. And sure enough, he hung around with Jimmy Durante for three or four days. This is the time when John Barrymore is reputed to have started his famous taxicab ride from Baltimore all the way to Denver or Kansas City, an incident that intrigued the country at the time. This incident, among others, made it an especially happy and rewarding intact bill. We were all sorry when it ended.

Jimmy Durante went back to New York; John Barrymore went by taxi to either Denver or Kansas City, and we returned to New York City also. Later on we saw Jimmy Durante frequently when we were working at Jimmy Kelly's. Jimmy Durante and Jimmy Kelly were good friends.

On Sunday nights the club featured famous songwriters who played requests from the audience of songs they had written. Their appearance made for a dazzling evening of music, especially when such famous persons as Irving Berlin appeared. Jimmy Durante loved those sessions and would frequently be there with his missus, sitting at his favorite table and listening intently. We had to go past him to do our number. With his customary friendliness and good humor, Jimmy Durante made a point of shaking our hands and saying what a great time we had in Baltimore and that he hoped we would do it again. Unfortunately, we never got the chance. He left a short time later for Hollywood and we stayed in New York. Incidentally, it is said he often went to another race track in California that was gaining in popularity. It had been built and promoted by Bing Crosby and was known as Delmar. It is there that he spent many of his last happy days. To me he was always the American "Cyrano de Durante" and he carried that persona with him on the stage. He was a wonderful, funny, warmhearted and beloved entertainer. God bless him.

"Good night, Mrs. Calabash. Wherever you are. . . . "

Along with other monumental comings and goings and leave takings during World War II, we always felt that Jimmy Durante personified that nostalgic phrase, "Kilroy was here." Jimmy Durante, too, left his mark as tens of thousands of American servicemen, particularly in the Air Transport Command, remembered and looked for that phrase stenciled or written or stamped or printed on walls or equipment wherever our troops were stationed. It reminded them that they were not alone, that someone had been there before them, had understood what they were going through and would be back again assuring them that:

"KILROY WAS HERE"

The variety theatre was a world of song, dance, mirth, and love.

—Hal Raymond

Some Wonderful Friends Along the Way

In those days, variety shows had an MC who was a capable entertainer in his own right.

Joey Bishop comes to mind. He was very well known at the start of television and later in movies. He fairly exuded good humor. He made us, the performers, feel ten feet tall when he introduced us and even taller when we came off. Another was Alan King. We didn't work with him personally, but we stood in the wings and watched him many times. He was the epitome of the suave, cigar smoking comedian and rightly deserved all the fame he received. And then there were two brothers who were English music hall comedians, Val and Ernie Stanton. They were truly excellent in the way they introduced, talked about and then signed off the acts when they were finished. They did so in a high class way and always added a lot of glamour to the show. We were on the road with them in the variety comedy, "The King's Scandals." And of course, there was Uncle Milty and his wonderful mother. The last time we worked with Uncle Milty was in Columbus, Ohio at the RKO Theatre. I think the unit was "Funsafire." No one could bounce a show along like Milton Berle. He was a great performer and a great Master of Ceremonies.

Of all the variety theatre performers I worked with or knew, I consider the greatest entertainer to be James Barton. This man was so gifted he could stay on the stage for hours and the audience would scream for him to come back if he threatened to leave the stage. He could do anything. He could dance like a pro; he could sing like a pro in all styless—swing, gospel, ballads, religious—and his sense of comedy was unbeatable. The last time we worked with him was at the Steel Pier in Atlantic City. As you may know, it extended out over the water. We had finished our act and were standing in the wings as usual to watch James Barton, when all of a sudden a hurricane struck. I think it was the devastating hurricane of 1938 called Carol.

In one shrieking instant it tore the roof off the theatre. Instead of allowing people to panic, as they started to do, James Barton continued his performance and held them in the grasp of his magic until ushers got them out in the safest way possible. It was a ravaging storm. But James Barton surmounted even the terrors of nature on the last time I ever saw him work. Later on he played the role of Jeeter Lester in "Tobacco Road," which ran for about four years.

Among other friends along the way who held a special place in my heart were the kinds of people who were the backbone of the variety theatre. They were the journeymen who gave it substance, vigor and grace. This was especially true of our dear and talented friends, Meryl Paige, Ken's wife, and Esther Paige, Roy's wife. Others include Johnny Matison, the choreographer who helped us develop our opening number done to the music of "Marie;" Roger Logan, singer and actor; Jack McCarver, the dancing instructor who taught us to stair dance; Ruth Best, the most gracious and capable booking agent in the greater Cincinnati area; Paul and Frank Reynolds and many others.

May and I were especially grateful to Mrs. Ramsey, the mother of our partner, Gladys Ramsey, for her kindness in letting us live in her apartment at 809 Ocean Avenue in Brooklyn just before the three of us began our long-time run at Jimmy Kelly's.

These tributes are in no way meant to disparage the brilliant young comedians of our own frenetic age in which they have to live and work. To mention just a few: Rita Rudner, Whoopi Goldberg, Robin Williams, Billy Crystal and others whose brilliance is acknowledged worldwide. Eddie Murphy is in a class by himself. His talent is so immense he can work in any vehicle and make you howl with laughter, a truly great comic talent who fits in with his times and, in my opinion, would fit in in any time.

These young people working under conditions of the present period demand a different style of comedy, which they handle in their own individually brilliant way.

And then there is Mr. Robert Hope, the Dean of all American comics who was imported by the city of Cleveland from England, and who I believe gave the sport of boxing, a short flight as Paddy McFarland which wasn't exactly his true calling. He became, instead, the King of all light entertainment and comedy. He deserves all the love, adulation, and, I might add, money he so richly deserves. He bridged all generations, as well as the immense contributions of time and talent he gave that were necessary and brave in entertaining our troops.

I would also like to recognize and name just a few of the gifted people and great acts we had the honor to work with in the variety theatre. They were: The Berry Brothers, Tic Tac and Toe, Leon Fields, Harry Rose, Three Little Words, Buck and Bubble, Wells Mordecai and Taylor, Clay Rambeau and others. These people, and others of their ilk, were the heart and soul of the variety theatre and gave countless hours of pleasure to the American public. God bless them all.

Epilogue

During World War II, Ken served as a producer with USO Naval troops at Treasure Island Naval Base co-producing its large productions for the Navy. After a brief stint in the Merchant Marines, I went back on the road with "Sons-of-Fun."

As the years went by and we found that we could no longer perform at our previous professional level, we left the variety theatre and joined forces as the real estate brokerage firm of Raymond and Paige, headquartered in New Haven, Connecticut. I said goodbye to the name "Hal"— which I used only in the variety theatre because it had been given to me by a numerologist (a big thing in those days) as a name that would bring me good luck, which it did. I went back to my full given name, Harry.

The persons and events described in this book are true, none of them are fiction.

As I recalled these memories, my second wife, Roby, put them down on paper as a testimonial to the spirit of variety theatre people and because she thought they would be of interest and value to my children and even, perhaps, to people who lived through those special times.